Magic When You Need It

150 Spells You Can't Live Without

Judika Illes

16pt

Copyright Page from the Original Book

This edition first published in 2008 by
Red Wheel/Weiser, LLC
With offices at:
500 Third Street, Suite 230
San Francisco, CA 94107
www.redwheelweiser.com

Excerpts from "Ride Lonesome, Ride Hard" by Peter Wolf and Will Jennings © 1998, used by permission of Pal-Park Music and Blue Sky Rider Songs.

Excerpts from "Lover Man" by Roger Ramirez, James Davis, and Jimmy Sherman © 1941, used by permission of Universal Music Corp.

Copyright © 2002. All rights reserved. No part of this publication may be reproduced or transmitted in any form or by any means, electronic or mechanical, including photocopying, recording, or by any information storage and retrieval system, without permission in writing from Red Wheel/Weiser, LLC. Reviewers may quote brief passages. Originally published as *Emergency Magic* in 2002 by Fair Winds Press, ISBN: 1931412014.

ISBN: 978-1-57863-419-4
Library of Congress Cataloging-in-Publication Data available upon request.

Cover and text design by Dutton & Sherman Design.
Typeset in Electra LH.

Printed in Canada
TCP
10 9 8 7 6 5 4 3 2 1

The paper used in this publication meets the minimum requirements of the American National Standard for Information Sciences—Permanence of Paper for Printed Library Materials Z39.48-1992 (R1997).

TABLE OF CONTENTS

introduction: magic when you need it	iii
section one: money and career	1
section two: love, sex, marriage, and children	35
section three: home	96
section four: trouble	121
a psychic shopper's guide	189
botanical classifications	195
acknowledgments	199
about the author	200
to our reader	201
Back Cover Material	202

For Greg Brandenburgh

Note: The recipes and spells in this book are based on ancient tradition and are for educational purposes only. The author and publisher assume no responsibility for any injury or damage caused or sustained while using the recipes and rituals described in this book.

introduction

magic when you need it

Conventional wisdom says that for every problem a logical solution exists. Sure sounds comforting, but let's face facts. In reality, life's worst-case scenarios are far more complex and complicated than that trite wisdom allows for, full of dramatic twists, turns and contradictions.

For example, what about that great new boyfriend of yours? He's everything you've ever dreamed of, except for one sticky detail: other women appreciate him too, and he appreciates their appreciation a little too much. What do you do? You don't want to leave him. You certainly don't want to lose him. You just want him to behave. What's the logical solution to that? Or maybe you're broke. There's an obvious solution to that, right? Get a job, get some money. Yet as anyone who's ever been there knows, that's much easier said than done.

So what do you do when life's worst-case situations demand urgent action, yet all the conventional responses are inadequate or nonexistent? What happens then? What are your alternatives? Do you give up? Roll over and play dead? Or do you turn to Earth's oldest existing system of crisis management: magic.

Oh, now wouldn't *that* be great, you think. After all, although one sometimes fantasizes about the fun magic can provide, it's when you're faced with dire crisis that the true need for enchantment arises. When your worst nightmare has transformed into your daily reality, wouldn't it be wonderful to just *magic* your way out of painful entanglements?

Well, you can, because in reality, magic is more than fantasies and wishful thinking.

Visualize your reactions to a personal crisis. A weight sinks to the pit of your stomach; a perpetual lump plagues your throat. You can't breathe. You can't think. Your mind has transformed into a broken record, endlessly returning to the source of your anxiety. Adrenaline rush elicits incessant fight-or-flight impulses.

The good news? Although you may be useless on the job, worthless at home, you've never been in better fighting form to accomplish genuine, working, solve-your-problems magic! The very same stress-induced reactions that make calm detachment so difficult are the ideal fuel for rescue magic. The magic of necessity is the most intense, effective magic of all, and stress, panic, worry, concern, intense fear and desire are your certified emergency-magic credentials. When you feel that adrenaline surging, you're also feeling your magical aptitude soaring.

After all, functional, dependable magic requires more than just lip service to a clever incantation or an investment in a few evocative props. For maximum effectiveness, magic demands nothing less of the practitioner than laser-intense, single-minded, borderline-obsessive mental focus. Nothing provokes that level of clarity and intensity of vision and desire more than a panic-worthy problem. The very same emotional and physiological responses to anxiety and dread that may have you overwhelmed can be channeled into magical mastery and problem solving. Rather than promoting passivity and hopelessness, magic encourages you to take the bull by the horns and realistically assess your situation and alternatives so that you can gain control of your destiny.

Magic's very existence stems from humanity's intense desire for crisis management. An ancient Egyptian papyrus known as *Instruction for Merikara,* believed to have been written approximately four thousand years ago, describes magic as a gift to humanity from the Creator "to ward off the blows of fate." Although the rapid natural degeneration of simple problems into bona fide worst-case scenarios stimulated the birth of magic, the sheer effectiveness of emergency enchantment is responsible for the very survival of magic. Despite centuries of deadly persecution and the brutal suppression of occult knowledge, magic has not gone away. Why not?

Because magic works.

Because faced with unrequited desire or an insoluble situation, quite often the enchanted solution is the only solution. In the face of a personal emergency, even the most ardent enemies of magic have found themselves relying on Earth's ancient wisdom.

A case in point springs from the Western world's most respectable book of metaphysics, the Bible. Saul, ancient Israel's first king, decreed practice of the shamanic and magical arts outlawed under penalty of death. Yet later, when facing his own worst-case scenario, where did Saul run to seek an emergency solution? Straight to the renowned witch of Endor, to beg her to come out of the retirement that he himself had imposed upon her. After some persuading, she relented and, in testimony to the effectiveness of emergency magic, conjured up the information from beyond the grave that Saul craved.

No spell is as effective as an emergency spell; no magic is as likely to work. You are in top magical form. But wait, hold on! Here's a fresh problem: Disaster often appears out of the blue. Magically speaking, are you prepared? When confronted with crises, are you ready to conjure up your own solutions? Despite all your magical aptitude and the dependability of emergency magic, odds are that you've found yourself all powered up, but clueless as to what to do.

THE MECHANICS OF MAGIC

What is magic, anyway? If you aren't already an experienced practitioner, you may be thinking, "I've never done this sort of thing before. Is it for real?"

As this is an emergency handbook, it's assumed that you may already be in crisis mode, with little time or patience for lengthy explanations or philosophy. For the magical virgins in our midst, suffice it to say that everything that occurs naturally on Earth or is created from naturally occurring components radiates various energies. Each of these distinctive energies may affect different departments of life. Magic is the conscious manipulation of these inherent energies.

Magic possesses a lot in common with cooking: follow the spell directions as you would a recipe. Of course, the greater your knowledge, the stronger and more consistent your personal power will be.

Tips for maximum magical effectiveness:

- No multi-tasking please! Magic is an old-fashioned art that demands 100 percent of your attention.
- Take your time—don't rush! Linger over spells. To give your intuition freedom to reveal your magical solutions, allow yourself as much space and quiet as possible. Once you've initiated a spell, pay special attention to your dreams, the context where inspiration so often appears and where prayers are often answered.
- Any time is the right time to perform emergency magic. Life has a way of letting you know when the right moment has arrived. However

if timing isn't critical, certain moments may be more auspicious than others.
- Magic performed to increase something (hair or money, for example) is best timed to begin with the waxing moon, the New Moon.
- Magic seeking to decrease or lose something (like debts or bad neighbors) is best timed to coincide with the waning moon, so start at the Full Moon.

Two types of emergencies exist:
1. Disasters that have already occurred.
2. Potential disasters.

Therefore, spells are either reactive or preventative. Take a tip from the Boy Scouts: Be prepared! Perform prevention spells before emergencies arise. Shouldn't everyone perform prevention spells? Well, a little prevention probably never hurt—but remember, genuine anxiety provides that added intensity that makes your spell extra-likely to work. If your anxiety level is low—let's say you're aware that a flu epidemic has hit town and you think you probably should take some preventative measures even though you aren't *really* concerned—you'll have to work harder to summon that clarity of vision and burst of desire.

THE COMPONENTS OF MAGIC

The spells in this collection derive from many places, cultures, and eras, ranging from ancient Egypt to modern New Orleans, from China to Arabia, from Jewish, Roman Catholic, and Vodoun traditions, among many other sources. Some spells were first recorded over a thousand years ago; others were devised to fit today's special circumstances.

With two exceptions, two spells have been offered for each of the seventy-five worst-case scenarios included in this book. This is meant to acknowledge both the vast treasure trove of magic spells from around the world and also that the needs of individual people can differ greatly. Choose the spell that resonates with you. In many cases, the spells complement each other wonderfully; if you'd like to try two spells simultaneously, that's great! On the other hand, if you find a spell distasteful for any reason, this is your magical intuition informing you that this isn't the right spell for you. Let your inner voice be your guide.

Although some spells have extremely detailed and explicit directions, others are more ambiguous: This is part and parcel of magic. There's room left in many spells for you to create your own personal imprint. When in doubt, access your intuition!

There is a gender component to a few spells. This reflects the reality that for centuries in many cultures, the needs of men and women have differed. Spells were created to fulfill these needs. In addition, according to traditional metaphysical wisdom, certain botanicals have different impacts on females and males, something like the proverbial chemical reaction. In some cases it is the spell-caster's gender that is specified; in others, it's the target of the spell that is significant.

No part of a spell is arbitrary: Every component must be carefully chosen for its specific power and influence. These components include colors, numbers, words, stones and botanicals, plus the elements: Air, earth, fire, and water.

Words hold tremendous power: choose them carefully and thoughtfully. Some of this book's spells suggest invocations or incantations. Use them if they feel comfortable and natural for you, and if they accurately convey your sentiments. It's crucial that you never feel silly, self-conscious or foolish at any point during your spell. Change the words if you like, so that they more accurately and intensely express your desires. Speak simply, clearly, and concisely. Your words need not wax poetic or rhyme.

Where can you find the ingredients for these spells? Some are common, everyday goods, like the brown paper specified in many spells; buy a pack of lunch bags or use supermarket shopping bags that you've cut to size. Other spells require ingredients as mundane as steak, sugar, and grapefruit.

Of course, depending upon your previous involvement with magic, some ingredients, like the magical roots High John the Conqueror or devil's shoestring, may seem very arcane indeed. Rest assured that most are inexpensively and easily obtained, once you know where to look. It is quite likely that a store selling witch supplies is conveniently located near you. If not, some reputable vendors are listed in "A Psychic Shopper's Guide" near the end of this book.

Items frequently used in emergency magic include the following:

Lodestones: Magnetic iron ore, these stones are used to magnetically draw your heart's desires straight into your hands. Used in spells for love and money, their recorded use goes back over a thousand years. Alexander the Great issued them to his troops for success and good fortune. Lodestones get tired. Their power needs to be replenished periodically. Traditionally, they're "fed" once a week by sprinkling them with iron shot, the fine iron filings also known as *magnetic sand.*

Botanicals: The powers of the plant realm manifest themselves through herbs and roots, essential oils, and flower essence remedies. Although most magical action occurs on spiritual planes, botanicals are the ancient basis of all medical systems. Truly a holistic power, botanicals affect people on every possible level: emotional, spiritual, and also physical. Every attempt has been made in this book to use botanicals that are safe for most people or to note when danger exists. However, if you possess any physical vulnerability, such as high blood pressure or a suppressed immune system, it is imperative that you verify whether a botanical will aggravate your condition. The scientific Latin names of the botanicals called for in this text have been provided at the end of the book to assist you with verification. Pregnant or nursing women, as well as those actively attempting to conceive, should verify every botanical prior to use. Botanicals can exert a profound physical influence when applied topically as well as when taken internally.

According to conventional wisdom, there's an exception to every rule, and *flower essence remedies* are the botanical exception. Descendents of alchemists' potions, flower essence remedies work their magic purely on the spiritual and emotional planes. They are gentle and safe for all to use, including children and animals. The names of the flower essence remedies cited in this book are followed by their manufacturer's name in parenthesis, for example, Mugwort Flower Essence Remedy (FES). Information on how to locate these manufacturers and their products may be found in the *Psychic Shopper's Guide* of this book.

Essential oils are not true oils. Instead they are highly concentrated plant extracts carrying an intensive dose of a plant's therapeutic and magical powers. Handle these extracts with care: They must be diluted in a real oil, such as apricot kernel, castor, or olive oil, before use.

Flower essence remedies and essential oils sound similar and are sometimes packaged in similar fashion but they are completely different vehicles for harnessing botanical power and must not be confused. Essential oils have profound physical as well as emotional and spiritual effects; flower essence remedies operate solely on a vibrational level. To underscore this difference, essential oils are sometimes described as the "life blood" of a plant while flower essence remedies, on the other hand, are believed to contain the plant's aura. Essential oils and flower essence remedies complement each other but are not interchangeable.

Some spells specify the quantities of the botanicals required, but many do not. In those cases, put your intuition and sense of smell to work by playing with the proportions until they feel, look, and smell right to you!

Spirits: It's almost impossible to completely divorce spirituality from true magic. This is where your personal beliefs come into play. All spells are most effective when accompanied by sincere prayer, but where that prayer is directed and to what or whom is entirely up to you.

No people, religion, or culture holds the monopoly on magic. Every culture in the history of Earth possesses magical traditions, whether they're currently practiced or not. Certain spells are affiliated with specific spirit beings because, in the manner of patron saints, these spirits are specialists in certain areas of life. When you approach them for help, you are requesting assistance from the world's top consultants in their feld. Always be respectful!

Several spells refer you to a specific spirit. To maximize the spell's effectiveness, you may want to learn more about the spirit than space allows for here. After all, it's often easier to request a favor from an intimate friend than from a stranger. If you'd prefer to substitute the deity of your choice, that's fine, too.

If you'd like to incorporate spiritual petition into your magic but are unsure as to whom to approach, the archangels are the most consistently accessible and helpful spirits of all. Request assistance from:
- *Raphael* for help with health issues
- *Michael* when protection is needed
- *Gabriel* when you just desperately need a miracle
- *Uriel* when you need information

Spells take many forms and styles:

Baths: Water's cleansing, protective, replenishing powers are infused with the powers of specific botanicals. Immerse yourself and absorb the power.

Spiritual petition: A temporary shrine is usually erected to signal that the spirit's presence is welcome and requested. Colors, numbers, and fragrances are manipulated to reflect the particular spirit's tastes. Manipulation of color and fragrance as well as the offering of very specific gifts or "meals" to the spirit serves to attract attention to you and your situation. Consider your shrine to be the equivalent of a spiritual SOS sign.

Candle burning: Candle magic, known as the philosophy of fire, transmits your secret wishes into the atmosphere where they can be transformed into reality. Different spells call for different candles. Occult stores and *botanicas* sell a vast variety of candles in many shapes and colors, each intended to achieve a specific goal. A spell may request a candle of a specific shape or color; if the proper candle is unavailable, however, a plain white candle may always be substituted.

Candles are more effective if personalized prior to burning. In magical parlance this is known as "dressing the candle." This is accomplished by embellishing the candle, usually by carving names, symbols and wishes into the wax. Any sharp-edged implement may be used as a tool: Rose thorns are traditional, but pens, skewers, and craft knives are also effective. You may also rub the candle with fragrance oils to adjust the aroma. *It is crucial that you remain aware of fire safety at all times. Candles must always be supervised; never leave burning candles unattended. Magic is never an excuse to challenge nature.*

Some candle spells include specific directions for how long a candle should be burned, but others do not. Adapt spells to suit your needs and circumstances. Unless otherwise specified, it is not necessary for a candle to burn in its entirety in one uninterrupted stretch. Feel free to extinguish your flame whenever it becomes necessary. In fact, burning a candle in increments may even be a bonus: Each time you relight the flame is another opportunity to reiterate your wish.

Condition oils: At the dawning of the twentieth century, as life became increasingly urbanized, people stopped gathering their own roots, growing their own herbs, and shaping their own candles. In the United States, the home of enthusiastic capitalism, an industry developed to supply spiritual and occult needs. Specific emergency formulas known as condition oils were developed, codified, and given catchy, dramatic names like *Fiery Wall of Protection* and *Follow Me, Boy!* to reflect American tastes and attract consumers.

Don't let the fun names and their relatively recent heritage make you underestimate their power: Condition oils are powerful magical concoctions with deep historic roots. Many of the Hoodoo workers responsible for naming and formulating these oils were also serious scholars of magical history. Although as far as we know, the ancient Egyptians didn't call it *Command and Compel Oil,* the roots of that basic formula, for example, can be recognized in surviving magical papyri.

Because condition oils were invented specifically to quickly deal with life's exigencies, this book relies upon them heavily. Simple, goal-oriented, and functional, they are emergency magic at its best. Although the formulas are somewhat generic, in the same way that every mother's chicken soup reflects her own tastes, traditions, budget, and available materials, so variations in condition oil formulas exist.

Unfortunately, the oils available commercially are rarely the best. If spells are to work, proper ingredients must be used. Disreputable manufacturers may put little more than colored baby oil and water in their products. To guarantee utmost power, it's best to mix up your own. Recipes for some of the most popular condition oils appear in a formulary following this introduction. Other formulas are given throughout the book. It is sometimes less expensive to buy ready-made condition oils, but choose them with care. If you're looking for a curio, purchase the cutest bottle. If you want your spells to work, buy oils and ingredients only from reputable vendors. See "A Psychic Shopper's Guide" near the end of this book for some suggestions.

Products of the body: The most precious, most powerful magical ingredients cannot be purchased in either a supermarket or a specialty store. They are priceless and must be handled with care. The products of the human body—assorted intimate fluids, strands of hair, nail clippings, and skin scrapings—are the traditional, vital components of crisis magic, and no substitutes exist.

A crucial point: Remember, magic is intended to solve and eliminate problems, not create further emergencies. Many of the spells in this book are truly ancient, but while human emotions and desires remain consistent over time, situations, circumstances, and concerns evolve over the ages. It is vital that you do not use spells that utilize bodily fluids in any way if you have a disease that can be transmitted via those fluids, for example, HIV infection, AIDS, or hepatitis. Instead, use an alternative spell to achieve your goals without endangering the health of others or of your own karma.

A COUPLE OF CAVEATS

If you're new to magic, it's crucial that you understand that its core philosophy revolves around the statement, *Do what you will, but harm none.*

I appreciate that you're desperate and you're willing to do *anything* to resolve your dilemma. Perhaps your situation scares you enough to make it seem that extreme solutions might be necessary. Perhaps other sources have recommended solving emergencies by performing blood sacrifices—killing birds or animals—as propitiatory offerings. Remove that thought from your mind right now. Instead of solving problems, you will only be creating new ones, adding even heavier baggage to your already overwhelming load.

There is no magic that requires you to harm another creature. There are modern spiritual traditions that do involve rituals of sacrifice, as all traditions did at one time. However, no tradition, modern or historical, permits a layperson to perform these sacrifices. Years of stringent initiation are required before permission is granted. Don't let desperation cloud your judgment!

As you flip through this book, you'll see spells that include ingredients like deer's tongue and Dragon's Blood. Never fear; these are botanicals, one and all. Many botanicals' nicknames tell us something about their powers: Deer's tongue, the lawyer's friend, encourages eloquence, while Dragon's Blood resin is a fiery agent of protection.

A few spells in this book do call for meat, in particular for various cuts of beef. If meat is part of your diet, then purchase those ingredients exactly as you would purchase them for a dinner recipe.

Another magical tenet is that every action possesses a boomerang effect. Your actions return to you multiplied manifold. In other words, spells performed for benevolent reasons will eventually bring happy returns. Spells that spring from malevolence bear the seeds of even greater problems.

Be very careful. Emergency situations and emergency magic touch on our deepest, most desperate desires. Because many of these spells involve controlling the will, desires, and destiny of others, they balance on a razor's edge between benevolent and malevolent magic. It's no accident that the most popular ingredient in this book is an oil called *Command and Compel.*

Before initiating any spell, it's always wise to closely examine your motivating intent. Consider, for example, a spell for getting rid of your daughter's boyfriend. Why do you want him gone? Ideally, this spell is intended to protect your daughter from harm and grave danger. Perhaps you have good reason to believe that her new boyfriend is a serial rapist, who's twenty years older than he's telling her. She's sixteen and won't listen to a word you say. Are you justified in using this spell? Absolutely.

But maybe the spell isn't really about him; maybe it's about your need to exert control over your daughter, and no man on Earth would meet with your approval. Maybe you just don't like his haircut, or maybe you'd prefer that his parents' financial portfolio was a little larger. Do you see? The situation has changed entirely. Will the spell work anyway? Yes, it very well may, but rather than diverting disaster, you'll be initiating and perpetuating an endless stream of crises.

Beware of the common cultural misconception of magic as something supernatural, something completely separate from real life that will somehow save you from real life. Just because magic can't be explained scientifically doesn't mean it isn't part of real life. It's crucial to understand that magic isn't separate from real life; it's a complementary art that works best when it's fully integrated into real life for enhancement and reinforcement. Both magical and conventional methods are enhanced and empowered when they are integrated together. Magic is never an excuse to behave stupidly. In other words, taking a magical approach to treating illness doesn't necessarily eliminate the need for a doctor, too.

An old Jewish story best illustrates this point:

> Panting, out of breath, a man runs desperately to his local miracle-working rabbi, exclaiming, "My house is on fire! Please help me, quick!" Instantly, the rabbi proffers his renowned staff, intricately carved with Kabbalistic

symbols. "Run fast, take this back to your home," he tells the man.

"Use this staff to draw seven circles around the house, surround those with seven magic squares, then stand back and pray to God to save your home!" As the man grabs the staff and turns to run home, the rabbi shouts after him, "And you know, water wouldn't hurt, either! Yes, before you do anything else, throw some water on the fire! As much water as you can!"

Magic is meant to empower you, to develop your hidden reservoirs of strength, insight and endurance. It's not a crutch. Magic won't do your work for you; instead it enhances the effects of other actions required of you, increasing your chances of success. You can create the most powerful employment charm in the world but if you don't show up for the job interview, it's useless.

Consider this modern fable:

Desperately broke yet exceedingly righteous, Susan decided that her only possible economic salvation was a big win in the lottery. Integrating magic and spirituality, she sprinkled ground pepper and cinnamon in every corner of her spartan home and began to pray. She petitioned the angels intensely; she reminded God of her many good deeds. Lottery night came and went: no win. Susan prayed harder, petitioned longer. The next lottery drawing came and went, but still she didn't win. By the third week, she was desperate and bitter and had taken to loudly castigating God and the angels for their lack of support and protection. Finally exhausted, Susan collapsed, wherein there was a sudden, intense flash of light and a majestic voice spoke from above: "Susan! We're doing the best we can! Work with us! Buy a damn lottery ticket!"

The very last caveat highlights a crucial, but subtle point: A fine balance exists between allowing fate to take its course and using magic to maintain control over your destiny.

Unfortunately, life doesn't always take the gentlest, kindest approach when teaching us needed lessons for which we may be grateful years later. There are times when it is best and absolutely necessary to challenge fate and demand control over your destiny. On the other hand, sometimes the most positive action you can take is to try to remain calm and ride out disasters with as much dignity and honor as you can master. In the words of singer Peter Wolf:

> *When you feel like life is breaking you,*
> *You've gotta go where the road is taking you*

Sometimes, wonderful, great fortune unexpectedly emerges phoenix-like from the ashes of disasters. Sometimes a crisis is required to spark needed transformation and growth. Sometimes, especially in matters of career and romance, loss is necessary to make room for new, happier, more fulfilling ventures. Every once in a while, Mother Nature knows better than you do what really is best for you.

Then again, sometimes not. Sometimes a disaster is truly a disaster that must be resolved or avoided at any cost. Consider carefully and decide for yourself.

YOUR MAGICAL EMERGENCY KIT

A Formulary of Condition Oils

Banishing Oil: Grind cinnamon, black pepper, cayenne pepper, salt, and sulfur powder together. Add roughly one tablespoon of the mixture to an ounce of castor oil and shake.

Command and Compel Oil: Grind one teaspoon of powdered sweet flag (also known as calamus) with one teaspoon of powdered licorice root. Add the powder to an ounce of castor oil and blend.

Crown of Success Oil: Blend essential oils of bay, frankincense, sandalwood, and vetiver into a jojoba oil base.

Fiery Wall of Protection Oil: Add one teaspoon of Dragon's Blood incense and one teaspoon of sea salt to one ounce of castor oil. Add five drops each of the essential oils of frankincense and myrrh. Shake the bottle vigorously to blend.

Van Van Oil: The most beloved oil of all, Van Van ideally is blended from five Asian wild grasses: citronella, gingergrass, lemongrass, palmarosa, and vetiver. Include as many of these grasses as you can to make your formula more powerful, but using lemongrass alone is adequate. Use either dried botanical powders or essential oils or a combination. Once the grasses are blended, mix them into a combination of castor and jojoba oil. Enhance the power of Van Van by adding a lodestone to the bottle, thus transforming it into *Lucky Lodestone Oil.*

Florida Water: This isn't an oil, it's a cologne, an agent of purification and a frequent component of magical spells.

16 ounces of distilled water

2 ounces of vodka or Everclear[1]
6 drops of essential oil of bergamot
6 drops of essential oil of lavender
2 drops of essential oil of clove bud

---

[1] Florida Water is for external use only, definitely not for consumption. Vodka or Everclear are recommended as ingredients only because these alcohols are comparatively scent-free and thus will not interfere with the aromas of the accompanying essential oils.

section one

money and career

Financial concerns are a great place to start because, while it's true that money won't buy happiness, the lack of it sure can spark and aggravate any other emergency!

general principles

• Use the colors green, gold, and yellow to draw prosperity toward you.

• Incorporate the numbers two and three into your spells as they encapsulate the concepts of doubling and increase.

• Lodestones allegedly draw life's riches towards you, as does the root charm High John the Conqueror.

• Because its color is a rich gold, jojoba is the oil of choice for money spells. Clear jojoba has been bleached; its power is broken.

• Appropriately, there are an abundance of spirits of prosperity! Hotei, the Chinese spirit of wealth, is particularly friendly and generous.

get cash fast

Some problems are very basic, like you need money now!

If you're desperate for a specific sum of money, this spell sends out an SOS to the universe for immediate financial aid.

SHOPPING BAG FULL OF CASH

1. Cut a square from a brown paper bag. Write the exact amount you need in the center.
2. Dress a green candle with essential oils of basil and bergamot.
3. If you're so inclined, petition the spiritual power of your choice to rescue you from your dire predicament.

Place the paper under the candle. Burn the candle daily for fifteen minutes at a time while petitioning, praying, and affirming your request until the specified amount is accumulated.

SHI SHI OIL

An old Hoodoo formulation, *Shi Shi Oil* has earned a reputation for putting poverty on the run and attracting wealth to the wearer—fast!

Shi Shi's basic formula is a blend of angelica root, bay leaves, and cloves. You may use either dried botanicals or essential oils.

1. If using dried herbs, grind them together using a mortar and pestle.
2. Add one tablespoon of the resulting powder to one ounce of jojoba oil, or add four drops of each essential oil to an ounce of jojoba. If you've used dried herbs, it may be necessary to shake vigorously to distribute them throughout the oil. If you've used essential oils, gently roll the sealed bottle to blend them.

- Rub *Shi Shi Oil* into your hair and onto the palms of your hands.
- Add it to your bath for extra intensity: Light a green candle

and visualize yourself prosperous, secure, and happy.
- Essential oil of clove can really irritate your skin. You may need to dilute the blend further by increasing the quantity of jojoba oil. Essential oil of angelica is a photosensitizer; avoid contact with direct light for 12 hours after its use.

***

get a loan

The crux of this dilemma is that you need someone to be generous toward you, and that person may have (let's be frank!) very good reasons not to be. Both spells are most effective when you apply for the loan in person.

HAND ME THE MONEY!

This spell is reputed to loosen up tight pockets and induce random acts of kindness.

1. Place a whole orris root in a small jar and cover it with jojoba oil.

2. Add 12 drops each of the essential oils of lavender and clary sage.
3. On the night prior to applying for the loan, add some of the oil to a tub filled with warm water and bathe. Inhale the fragrance and concentrate on success!
4. Just before applying for the loan, rub a bit of the oil onto the palms of your hands.
5. Do not wash your hands before you can shake hands with the loan officer.

PROSPERITY WALK

Sometimes hands work the magic, but sometimes it's the feet!
1. Blend essential oils of basil, frankincense, myrrh and sandalwood in a tablespoon of sweet almond oil. Only a very few drops of each oil are needed.
2. Before applying for the loan, anoint your heels with the oil. (This oil can be very effective when applying for a job, too!)

***

have your debts forgiven

You must understand that there is no spell that allows you to welsh on your debts without repercussion. There is such a thing as karma. However, perhaps you've found yourself in a critical financial bind. You'd love to pay off all your debts if you could, but you can't, and there's little hope for the situation changing in the foreseeable future. Now that's a whole different set of circumstances...

SPIRITUAL BOARD OF DIRECTORS DECISION

In Chinese tradition, tremendous efforts are made to collect (and pay!) all money owed before the lengthy New Year period ends. If it can't be collected by then, debts *may* be forgiven, as it's inauspicious to carry debt into the New Year.

You will need a statue of Hotei, the fat, laughing Lord of Wealth, and of beautiful Kwan Yin, Goddess of Mercy. (Lacking statues, designate something, perhaps candles, to represent them.)

1. Place them side by side, with a dish of uncooked rice between them.
2. Carve your name, birthday, and the amount of money you need to comfortably pay off your debt onto a white or green votive candle. Place the candle on the bed of rice and light it.
3. Speak to Hotei and Kwan Yin. Explain your debt situation and tell them you are leaving it in their capable hands.
4. Designate a date, by which time Hotei and Kwan Yin must reveal their decision to you. You must contact your creditors by that date. Respectfully and honestly explain your dire circumstances and offer to pay an amount that you can realistically afford.
- Should Hotei bless you with riches, you must promptly pay off your debts.

- If this blessing is not to be, request that Kwan Yin transmit compassion to your creditors.

LETTER OF MERCY

1. Carve your name, birthday, and the sum of money that you owe into a white candle.
2. Dress the candle with *Tranquility Oil* (Roman chamomile, lavender, and ylang ylang) in an olive oil base.
3. Write a letter to your creditor. Apologize for the delay, explain your circumstances, and detail the repayment plan that's ideal for you. Sign and date the letter.
4. Place the letter beneath the candle. Make your wish and light your candle.
5. When the candle burns out, dispose of any remaining wax or paper fragments outside your home. (Remember, this is a spirit letter, not intended for other humans to read. If the letter isn't destroyed during the

burning process, make sure that it's illegible prior to disposal.)
6. Make an honest effort to repay a portion of your debt.

***

collect your debts

Watch out! These rank among the most powerful spells. Be absolutely sure that there's no doubt that you're entitled to the money.

GREEN DEVIL REPOSSESSION SERVICE

Pay me back or there'll be the devil to pay! Green candles shaped like little devils are burned to get cash fast and to have loans repaid. *Command and Compel Oil* is a powerful formulation that allegedly forces others to do your bidding. Combine the two to get your money back.

1. Add five drops of essential oil of bergamot to *Command and Compel Oil*.

2. Carve your debtor's name and the sentence, *"Give me my money!"* on a green devil candle.
3. Rub the candle with *Command and Compel Oil* while simultaneously concentrating on your dilemma.
4. Write the debtor's name nine times on a square of brown paper. If he or she uses pseudonyms or multiple names, write them all. Leave no name to hide under!
5. Write the phrase *"Give me my money!"* over each of the names, in the process crossing the names out.
6. Anoint each corner of the paper with a drop of *Command and Compel Oil.*
7. Place the paper beneath an overturned saucer and place the candle on top.
8. Light the candle and, as it burns, speak directly to the candle, demanding the return of what is rightfully yours. Visualize that you are speaking to your debtor, if this is effective for you. Say

whatever is in your heart; however, the traditional incantation goes something like this:

(Borrower's name), give me my money now!
You owe it to me. I need it. Give it to me.
You can't rest until you give it to me!
Whenever you see the color green, you're thinking about the money you owe me
Whenever you hear the clink of metal, whether from coins or forks or knives, you're thinking about the money you owe me
You can't sleep until you give me my money,
You can't eat until you give me my money,
You can't have sex until you give me my money.

(You get the gist. Make the effects as specific as possible and as relevant to the personal situation as possible.)
Give me my money or you will burn.

1. Remove the paper from under the saucer, singe it a little in the fire, and then, with your fingers, pinch out the candle.
2. Repeat this ritual for seven days.
- At some point during those seven days, you must attempt to contact the borrower and calmly ask for the return of your money. If any portion is repaid, consider the spell concluded. Offer your thanks to the debtor and helpful spirits alike.
- If by the eighth day, however, no money is forthcoming, light the candle again. Hold the paper in the flame and allow both the candle and paper to burn completely. Repeat the invocation but change the last line to:
*You have my money,
Now burn!*

SEE A PENNY, PICK IT UP

Because the green devil spell comes so close to a hex, it's necessary to contact your borrower. You must offer the opportunity for the debtor to save him- or herself by repaying you, although by no means are you required to mention the spell. If you would prefer a more indirect, anonymous approach, the following spell is also allegedly very effective.

1. Soak a penny in *Command and Compel Oil* for twenty-four hours, preferably while exposed to the light of the full moon.
2. Glue the coin to the middle of a square white paper card.
3. On the card, write (in Dragon's Blood ink, if possible), *"You owe me. Now pay me!"*
4. Mail it to your debtor. It isn't necessary to sign the message or make any other contact, although, as it's likely that he or she owes money to many people, it might be in your best interests to somehow identify which debt is being called in!

***

collect your child support

This is the most profound debt of all as it involves issues and obligations larger than money alone. If collecting child support is your personal crisis, rest assured that a host of sympathetic spirits exist to battle on your behalf.

MADAME EZILI'S COLLECTION SERVICE

The spirit most easily roused to action is probably Ezili Danto, the fierce Vodoun champion of single mothers. A hardworking single mother herself, she is intensely devoted to her own daughter, Anaïs, whom she supports single-handedly. Madame Ezili has absolutely no patience with deadbeat dads. No need to explain your situation to her; she already knows all about it.

Appeal to her for assistance in getting the money you're owed and also to increase your financial independence so you won't need it so desperately.

1. Designate a small, flat space—a table or countertop—as your altar. The colors red and/or

white will catch Ezili Danto's attention.
2. Set out an offering of a glass of 151 (overproof) rum and a glass of *Florida Water,* side by side.
3. Speak to her from your heart and tell her what you need.

MYRRH MONEY POT

Once upon a time, myrrh was one of the most expensive items on Earth. Less pricey today, although no less precious, myrrh can be used to open tight pockets. The fragrance also evokes the presence of the powerful Egyptian spirits Hathor and Isis, two eternally stalwart protectors of women and children.
1. Although no doubt he owes you big bucks, what you need to do is get him to voluntarily hand you a single coin. The value of the coin may be as little as a penny. How you maneuver this is up to you.
2. Wrap a blue thread around the coin.

3. Drop the coin into a small, lidded glass jar and anoint it with essential oil of myrrh. Close your jar securely and keep it safe in a secret hiding place.

Whenever you receive a payment, feed the jar by adding a bit more myrrh.

***

turn around a bad investment

Is it beginning to feel like you've bought the Brooklyn Bridge? It sure seemed like a great deal at the time. But now it's a lead weight dragging you down and, unfortunately, it looks like you're stuck with it. Use magic to transform that investment.

ALLSPICE, ALL FORTUNE

Allspice berries encourage financial prosperity through business ventures; their use is specifically indicated for poor investments. Vervain manipulates the wheel of fortune to turn in your favor.

1. Place a generous handful of dried vervain, three cinnamon sticks, and a tablespoon of whole allspice berries inside a clear jar.
2. Pour boiling water over the botanicals until they're covered.
3. When the infusion cools, strain out the plant material and add five drops each of the essential oils of patchouli and vetiver to the infusion.
4. Add most of the infusion to your bathwater. Also, put a small amount in a spray bottle and lightly spray anything related to your investment.

INVESTMENT EMPOWERING CHARM

1. Tie a tonka bean and a chunk of frankincense resin together with green thread.
2. Wrap them in yellow or gold cloth, rolling the cloth toward you.

3. Store the charm with papers or other items representing your investment.

***

increase business now

Trouble in the marketplace is a worst-case scenario that transcends time, place, and culture. Appropriately then, remedial spells abound, both ancient and modern.

BUSINESS IN THE BAG!

A particularly ancient spell, this one is derived from the Middle East.
1. Carefully collect dust from an anthill.
2. On a piece of fine-quality stationery—the type you'd use if your business was all that it should be—write your business goals as plainly and specifically as possible. Use the present tense. For instance, write "I sell 1,000 units every week." If a particular image symbolizes success for you, draw it. Fold

the paper into a tight, small square.
3. Place the dust, the paper, and a small lodestone inside a small beaded bag and hang it where you conduct your business.

BETTER BUSINESS FLOOR WASH

Van Van Oil evokes passionate responses from practitioners. Dependable and fragrant, powerful and versatile, *Van Van Oil* allegedly turns poor luck into the best, and poor investments into sources of pride and prosperity.

1. Add Mrs. Stewart's Bluing, *Van Van Oil,* vinegar, ground cinnamon, and *Florida Water* to a bucket of water. (See *Van Van Oil* and *Florida Water* recipes.)
2. Wash the floor of your place of business with this mixture. Pretend that you are a customer entering the premises: Start washing at the business's entrance.
3. Then, move on to the interior. Wash each of the four corners

first, then work toward the center of the room. Continue until all areas have been cleansed in this fashion.

***

get a job

You're not trying to be unemployed! You'd love to work. Why is finding work such a challenge?

THE NINE-DAY EMPLOYMENT SEARCH

This spell is reputed to work within nine days, but for maximum effectiveness, you must simultaneously look for work intensively.

1. Tie a cinnamon stick and a High John the Conqueror root together with either green or gold thread.
2. Anoint the botanicals with *Three Kings Oil* (frankincense, myrrh, and spikenard) and then place them in a red-flannel drawstring bag.

3. Every morning before you go out to search for work, feed your botanical charm a little *Three Kings Oil*.

If your situation remains unchanged after nine business days, it's time to reassess your plans and explore alternatives.

THE LONG-TERM CAREER SOLUTION

1. On a piece of brown paper, make a list of all of the obstacles to your success. Include everything, every person, every circumstance, and every situation that crosses and opposes your success. Try to be as specific as possible.
2. You will need a black candle to represent each of your obstacles. Carve each obstacle on its own black candle. Repeat the phrasing that you used on the brown paper. As each obstacle will have its own candle, you may write as much as you need.

Carve words into the whole candle if necessary.
3. Odd numbers are most powerful, but if you can't honestly avoid having an even number of obstacles, include a final candle upon which you may carve an abbreviated list of all your hurdles.
4. Dress each candle with *Banishing Oil*.
5. Burn one candle a night, scorching the paper each time. Wait until the final night to burn the whole paper in its entirety.
6. After the final candle has been burned, light a green or gold success candle (green if cash is your crucial motivator, gold if it's success or prestige).
7. List everything that you desire from a job, as specifically as possible, on another piece of brown paper and burn it simultaneously with your success candle.

***

make a great first impression

You have one chance, one opportunity, maybe only five minutes to create the right impression. Back yourself up with these spells.

PERSONAL MAGNETISM MAGNET

1. Obtain a small lodestone and a High John the Conqueror root.
2. Dress both with a few drops of *Attraction Oil* (allspice, cinnamon, and frankincense).
3. Anoint the corners of a dollar bill with *Van Van Oil*.
4. Rolling the bill toward you, roll the root and the lodestone up inside the bill. Visualize charisma and good fortune rolling into your life. Tie the money roll with a golden thread.
5. Place the charm in a red-flannel drawstring bag and carry it with you, keeping it within easy contact of your skin.

PERSONAL POWER POWDER

1. Combine a teaspoon of ground cinnamon and a half-cup of cornstarch.
2. Add twelve drops of essential oil of peppermint, stir, and allow the mixture to dry.
3. On the stove, gently blend a cup of honey into a quart of milk.
4. Draw a warm bath for yourself, add the milk and honey to it.
5. While in the bath, focus on your goals and all your finest attributes.
6. When you are done bathing, dry yourself with a clean white or purple towel and dust yourself with the powder.

Dust the powder on your skin again immediately before your appointment.

***

ensure a great job interview

You managed to get your foot in the door. Now you need to clinch the deal.

MAGNETIC ME

1. Feed a lodestone with iron shot (magnetic sand) and a few drops of *Van Van Oil*.
2. Wrap it in red flannel or place it in a small red-flannel bag and wear it next to your heart when you go to the interview. (Tuck it into your bra, pin it within your clothing or tape it to your skin.)
3. Take a deep breath, look your interviewer in the eye, radiate calm confidence, and focus on winning the job.

FREE PASSAGE TO THE SALT MINES

1. Whisper your goals and desires over some sea salt and then place the salt in your pocket before you go to the interview.
2. If you can, sprinkle a little of the salt on your interviewer's clothes without being observed. (Kiss the job goodbye if you are observed.) This action should

both help you get the job and be treated fairly by that person.
- If you are unable to actually sprinkle the interviewer, try to discreetly leave a sprinkling of salt in the office before you leave.
- Leaving traces of the salt on your interviewer or in the office increases the power of the spell, but if that turns out to be impossible, don't stress! Don't take undue risks. Just having the salt in your pocket should provide the success you need.

***

deliver a great speech

Oh, to possess eloquence! Sure, for some it's no big deal; but for others, public speaking is scarier than running into a burning building. Sometimes, it isn't the speaking itself that's so frightening, it's the awareness that so much rides upon a single performance.

CUP OF COURAGE

"I, Borage, bring Courage!" Or so goes the old English rhyme. The herb borage has an ancient reputation for providing cheerful courage while steeling heart and nerves. Use borage when a burst of bravery is desperately needed.

1. Squeeze the juice from a tangerine, lemon, or lime and mix with one-quarter cup of sugar.
2. Add one-quarter cup of borage and stir thoroughly. Let it steep overnight.
3. Strain the borage from the liquid and discard it.
4. Add the liquid to sixteen ounces of red wine and serve over ice, garnished with sliced oranges.

Depending upon your tolerance of alcohol, you can either drink your cup of courage right before your speaking engagement or you can drink it the night before. Toast your eloquence and success!

CRUCIBLE OF COURAGE

Found yourself in a jam? Let *Crucible of Courage Oil* assist you. It's a formula of extreme potency to be used when life issues you a frightening or dangerous challenge. If you're extremely timid, make this your daily perfume. It doesn't give you courage so much as help you to discover the reserves hidden deep within. Don't think you have any? *Crucible of Courage* is indicated particularly for those plagued by self-doubt and lack of confidence.

Blend essential oils of black pepper, frankincense, lavender, sandalwood, and vetiver until the fragrance suits and soothes you. Dilute the mixture in jojoba oil. The aroma may change following dilution: adjust by adding more essential oils, as necessary.

Add a drop of borage flower essence remedy for enhancement (available from FES, Green Hope Farm, and Pegasus Products).

> The herbs deer's tongue and five-finger grass bestow eloquence when carried in the pocket, as does

> the gemstone lapis lazuli when worn at the throat.

***

up the ladder: get a raise or promotion

Stuck in a rut? Afraid of being passed over? This time, you desperately need that raise or promotion!

CROWN OF SUCCESS

This condition oil allegedly guarantees success, especially in professional, academic, and military matters.

Blend essential oils of bay, frankincense, sandalwood, and vetiver into a jojoba oil base.

Add some oil to your bath once a week, or whenever you sense even the remotest possibility of a raise or promotion.

Rub some on your hands daily before departing for work.

PROMOTION CHARM BAG

1. Fill a red-flannel drawstring bag with the following botanicals:

   Five-finger grass (for success and so people will do favors for you)

   Dragon's Blood resin (to attract good fortune)

   Deer's tongue (for eloquence)

   Gravel root (to get that job or promotion)

   High John the Conqueror root for personal magnetism and best success

2. Anoint the bag with *Crown of Success Oil* and carry it in your pocket or in contact with your skin.

***

pass an exam

Okay, so you could have studied a little harder. Or maybe the jitters do bad things to your memory. Use these magical assists to help you ace the test!

BAY BACCALAUREATE

Did we mention the versatility of *Crown of Success Oil?* Use it to enhance your confidence, memory, and the likelihood of getting a great grade!

1. Carve your name, birthday, the date of your exam or deadline, and any other pertinent facts into a green skull candle. Dress it with *Crown of Success Oil* and burn it beside you while you study.
2. Anoint your forehead and hands with the oil prior to the exam. You may also anoint papers with *Crown of Success Oil* before you submit them to increase the odds for success.

MAGIC MEMORY AID

1. Sprinkle ground cinnamon and cloves into some honey—rosemary honey, if at all possible.
2. Add a few drops of pure vanilla extract.

3. Inhale the fragrance and let the dish sit beside you for a minimum of an hour while you're studying.
4. Just before the exam, slide a sprig of rosemary through the scented honey and rub it against the back of your neck.

***

get your boss off your back

You've been trying not to take it personally, but at this point, it's hard not to. Is going to work starting to feel like going to Hell?

SABOTAGE THE SABOTEUR!

Maybe your boss isn't entirely to blame. Maybe someone else is sabotaging your position or your good relationship with your boss.
1. Write the person's name three times on a square of brown paper.
2. Write your own name over each line, all the while chanting, "I cover you, I cross you."

3. Anoint the corners of the paper with essential oils of clove and lavender.
4. Fold it up and place it in a red-flannel drawstring bag along with some cumin seed and a devil's shoestring root to foil any malevolent acts directed at you.
5. Keep your charm in a safe, private place, preferably in the workplace, feeding it daily with a drop of essential oil of lavender for reinforcement.

BOSS FIX

This formulation is reputed to cause harassment to cease and to compel your supervisor to treat you with kindness, fairness, and generosity. (Okay, okay. At the very least it's supposed to make them keep their distance.) This is a very specific spell, targeted at one specific individual. If more than one person is causing you grief, repeat the spell per person.

1. Grind up chili powder, tobacco (unroll a cigarette; use your boss' favorite brand if he or she

smokes), and shredded, pulverized newsprint (your boss' favorite newspaper, if possible). During this process, visualize the success of your goal, *not* your fear of getting caught.
2. When you have a discreet moment and there's no one around to see you, sprinkle the powder across the doorway to the boss' office or, better yet, on or around his or her chair. No need to leave a big suspicious pile. A little *Boss Fix* goes a long way. The key is to place the powder so that your target is guaranteed to step over it.

section two

love, sex, marriage, and children

This is a broad category, the connection being that all of the situations pertain to matters of the heart. Romantic emergencies, in particular, differ from most crises in that the stimulus for action comes from desperate desire rather than from what some might consider true crisis. Yet the need for action is no less urgent.

general principles

- Incorporate the colors yellow, orange, and pink into your love spells.
- Although there are many, *many* spirits of love, Aphrodite and Oshun have consistently proven to be accessible and generous.
- The most powerful love numbers are five (because it belongs to Oshun), six (because that's Aphrodite's special number), and two (for obvious reasons).

- Use lodestones, orris root, and the aromas of rose and jasmine to attract and keep romance and true love.
- The same numbers work for marital issues, but substitute the color red.
- Pine and magnolias radiate marital bliss.
- Juno is the divine matron of marriage.
- For spells relating to children, substitute pink or any other color that has personal significance to your situation.
- Children have many spiritual guardians. Among the most potent and accessible are Kwan Yin of China and the Egyptians Isis and Bes.
- Rose quartz, coral, iron metal, and angelica root are auspicious for children.
- Five is the most powerful number of protection.

make yourself irresistible

Tired of being alone? Perhaps you don't have one special person in mind ... yet. You need to be able to look around, to have your pick of everyone available. Or maybe you need others to do your bidding? In short, you need to be irresistible.

CONSIDER ME A GODDESS RITUAL

Who is more irresistible than a goddess of love? Coincidentally or not, some of the most charismatic spirits of love are also master practitioners of the magical arts. Entrancing Aphrodite, Circe, and Oshun spin webs of desire and allure. This ritual asks them to share some of their spell-binding essence with you.

1. Carve each spirit's name at the top of her own yellow candle. There will be three candles in all.
2. Carve your own name and birthday three times on each candle, beginning at the base

and working your way toward the top.
3. Make your invocation:
Please Aphrodite, please Circe, please Oshun
Immerse me in your beauty, intelligence, and charm
Bearing your essence, I am irresistible

4. Make offerings: a rose for Aphrodite, a dish of honey for Oshun (taste it first; Oshun accepts no untasted offerings), and a small toy lion for Circe.
5. Light the candles and draw a warm bath for yourself.
6. Smooth honey on your body, concentrating on a vision of yourself as charismatic and in control.
7. Enter the bath, allowing the honey to permeate the water.
8. After emerging from the bath but before you dress, prepare your charm: Anoint an orris root and cinnamon stick with neroli or petitgrain essential oils. Tie them together with a yellow satin

ribbon. Wrap up the little bundle in white, pink, or gold fabric and carry with you as needed.

Q PERFUME OIL

No one seems to remember what the *Q* in *Q Perfume Oil* stands for. However, this esteemed old Hoodoo formulation allegedly bestows the gift of irresistibility upon its wearer! There's only one way to find out for sure....

1. Add four drops of carnation absolute (similar to an essential oil), four drops of essential oil of myrrh, and one drop of essential oil of peppermint to one generous tablespoon of apricot kernel oil and blend gently.
2. Apply *Q Perfume Oil* to the body as needed.

***

make someone love you

At last! You've found your true love. Now here's the challenge: You need to be loved in return. These spells are most powerful when initiated on a New Moon Friday.

MAKE HIM LOVE YOU!

1. Blend honey, jasmine flower water, orange flower water, and rose water in a shallow saucer.
2. Place a pink votive candle in the center of the saucer.
3. With a pin or a rose thorn, scratch his name and yours, enclosed within a heart, on each of five sugar cubes.
4. Arrange the sugar cubes around the candle in the saucer.
5. Strongly visualize the fulfillment of your heart's desire and light your candle. For added intensification, repeat this ritual every night for five consecutive nights.

MAKE HER LOVE YOU!

1. Sprinkle a lodestone with one drop each of the essential oils of cardamom, frankincense, and sandalwood, plus a tiny bit of your sweat.

2. Wrap the lodestone in a red-flannel cloth, folding the cloth toward you.
3. Carry your charm in your pocket, within easy reach, until your next encounter.
4. When you see her, rub your hand on the lodestone packet.
5. Touch her with that hand immediately!

***

make love last: binding spells

You've finally found that special person you can't live without. You can't take a chance on your beloved finding another: he or she must be yours, forever! Use these spells to keep your lover spellbound.

CAFÉ D'AMOUR

Traditionally, if not always accurately, binding spells have been considered feminine concerns. Appropriately then, the ultimate binding ingredient is a single drop of menstrual blood served in a cup of coffee or a glass of wine. One taste and, so the legend goes, he (or she!) is yours for life! If you don't menstruate because you're male, menopausal, or otherwise, the next spell is reputedly very effective.

1. Snip off a tiny bit of your pubic and underarm hair.
2. Grind them together with fresh coffee beans and then brew.
3. Personalize that cup of coffee: add lots of sugar, cream, and/or chocolate. A dollop of Amaretto, Sambuca or similar liqueur wouldn't hurt, either.
4. Serve it with a smile.

'TIL DEATH DO US PART

Graveyard dust is a magic ingredient of ancient and worldwide renown. If you have the real thing, use it, preferably from the grave of a loved one who cares about you and will intercede for you from the other side. If that isn't possible, combine a little bit of fresh, clean dirt with some powdered patchouli and/or valerian. Sift it until it is very fine and bake it into a cake with lots of chocolate and cinnamon. Then feed it to him. If you can have him eating out of your hands, all the better.

***

make an unwanted lover leave

Oh, you got him, all right. Boy, did you get him! Now you can't wait to lose him—permanently!

MESSAGE IN A BOTTLE

1. Cut a small strip from the Unwanted One's clothing, preferably from his or her underwear or a sock. (Hold the laundry: unwashed clothes make your spell most likely to work.)
2. Stuff it into a clean, empty bottle and dispose of what's left of that piece of clothing. That means get it out of your house now!

3. On a piece of brown paper, write the Unwanted One's name plus the name of an extremely remote, faraway place. (That means far away from *you*. If you live in the middle of the South Pacific, then pick a spot somewhere in New York State.) Draw one circle around both names.
4. Add the paper to the bottle.
5. Now add one teaspoon each of salt, red pepper, and sulfur powder.
6. Let the bottle rest in a dark, quiet, lonely spot for nine days.
7. Toss the bottle in a stream or other running water. Walk away without looking back.
8. You should see results within nine days.

GET LOST PERFUME

In the days of the polio epidemic, vigilant mothers tied small bags of white camphor around their children's necks to keep illness at a distance. Use this technique to remove your own personal walking headache. Either place a lump of white camphor in red flannel and tie it around your neck the old-fashioned way, or anoint yourself with a drop of essential oil of white camphor.[2] Just be careful: It may keep others away, too!

***

make him be true to you

Oh, that cheating hound! You love him. Now if he could only keep his pants on! These spells will fix his zipper for him. They won't change his personality, though. Consider whether a spell to trade him in for a more committed lover might not be most beneficial in the long run.

THE LOVE LEASH

Is the possibility of his voluntary fidelity too ridiculous to even contemplate? The following spell is intended to cause selective impotence. Basically, it ties up his sexual desires

---

[2] Make sure it's white camphor; other types are toxic.

and aptitude and looses them only for you! All you need is a piece of smooth cotton string and him. Take as much time between steps as necessary.

1. Trim the string to match the length of his erect penis. (How you accomplish this is up to you. A suggestion: be inventive, make it a game. For the sake of the success of your spell, not to mention the future of your relationship and perhaps your own safety, DO NOT allow him to guess your intentions.)
2. Start a knot in the center of the string. In other words, form the loop for the knot, but don't pull it tight. Yet.
3. Hide the string but keep it close at hand (like maybe under your pillow or mattress, or in a pocket) until the appropriate moment arises.
4. Here's the challenge: have sex, then discreetly soak the string in his seminal emissions. It is CRUCIAL that fluids from only his body touch the string, not even a drop of your own, or the

spell will tie you up along with your lover. Make sure you use no intermingled love juices! Again, how you accomplish this is up to you; offering to dispose of a used condom may work.
5. Encourage him to fall asleep (whether it is before or after you soak the string is irrelevant).
6. When he is asleep, call his name.
7. When he answers, pull that knot tight!
- Keep your little love leash safe in a secret spot. You never have to repeat this spell from the beginning (with this particular man anyway); reinforce it as necessary by adding more knots and proceeding from step 6. For maximum effectiveness, carry the leash inside a conjure bag tied around your waist, hidden beneath your clothes.
- If you ever decide that this man is just too much trouble, it's best to be kind and remove all the knots from the string after your relationship's demise. (This also

stops him from hanging around you when you could be pursuing other opportunities!)

PLANT YOUR FEET AT HOME!

1. Offer to give him a pedicure. Make it romantic.
2. Begin by scraping off any dry skin, preferably from the heel.
3. Proceed as you wish, but preserve that skin!
4. The traditional method is to bury the skin under your doorstep as he sleeps peacefully in your bed. You may also sew it into a small dream pillow, which you then keep tucked under your own pillow at all times.

***

magic viagra

Too much sex isn't your problem. Oh no, quite the opposite! Well, thousands of years prior to the invention of Viagra, magic provided remedies, too.

THE KEY TO LOVE

An old Moroccan spell for impotence advocates obtaining seven keys from seven houses in seven towns, then heating them until they're red hot, preferably in an iron pan. Once this has been done, boiling water from seven different wells is poured over the keys and the man is exposed to the steam.

Reproduce it if you can, but in our time, it's difficult to find water from one well, let alone seven. Substitute seven sources of water for the seven wells. Don't use tap water. Instead, use pure spring water from seven different springs (bottled is fine.) Bathing appropriate areas with the metal-infused water, once it has cooled, may also be beneficial.

HAREM PERFORMANCE POTION

Renowned as the herb of increase, fenugreek's magical gifts include more than just increasing cash reserves and prosperity—a flamed harem remedy, an infusion of fenugreek was used by women to enhance their busts and by men to improve their sexual function.

1. Place two teaspoons of fenugreek seeds in a cup and cover with a cup of boiling water.
2. Steep for five minutes, then add a slice of lemon and honey to taste and drink. Try orange blossom or manuka honey for an additional aphrodisiac boost!

***

make him pop the question

You belong together. It seems so obvious to you that marriage is the logical next step. So why are you still singing the wedding bell blues?

WEDDING CANDLE

This popular figure candle, found in many occult-supply stores, depicts a conjoined man and woman—sometimes, but not always, dressed in wedding attire. (Sometimes they aren't dressed at all.) Though a wedding candle works best for this spell, you can substitute either:

- A male figure candle and a female figure candle[3]
- One pillar candle, in the color of your choice, to represent each of you

1. Create an altar of love, a small wedding shrine. Suggestions: decorate it with images from your dream wedding. Cut out photos from wedding magazines. Add the bride-and-groom wedding cake figurines that most closely resemble you and your beloved.
2. Carve your names (encircled within a heart), your birthdays, astrological signs, and maybe even the desired wedding date into each candle.

---

[3] If you use a pair of substitute candles (rather than one true wedding candle), it is crucial that the candles be placed so close together that as they burn, their waxes intermingle and become one.

3. Dress your candle with as many of the following essential oils as possible: gardenia, neroli or petitgrain, jasmine, pine, rose, and tuberose.
4. Light the candle. While it burns, focus on your goals.
5. When the candles have burned down, wrap all of the wax fragments in a silk scarf and put them in a safe place. It's time to broach the subject again!

QUEEN OF SHEBA

That King Solomon already had a hundred wives and countless concubines was immaterial. When the Queen of Sheba arrived from Ethiopia, bearing precious gifts, he knew she was the one. This spell relies on her repertoire of enchanting, seductive fragrances to enhance your own marital plans.
1. Obtain a sheet of paper suitable for a wedding invitation and a square of fabric suitable for a wedding gown.
2. In the center of the paper, draw the image of a single wedding

ring (a circle within another circle).

3. Write your name and your intended's in the center of the ring. If you plan to change your name after the marriage, include your future name as well.

4. Anoint the four corners of the page with *Queen of Sheba Oil:* three drops of essential oil of amyris, two drops of essential oil of cinnamon bark, three drops of essential oil of frankincense, three drops of essential oil of myrrh, three drops of rose attar, and two drops of essential oil of spikenard.

5. Tie up the paper together with an orris root and a piece of myrrh inside the square of fabric and place it beneath your pillow or mattress.

6. Dress the corners of the page every Friday until you receive your proposal.

***

make your mother-in-law love you

"Satan should be her name," sang Ernie K-Doe in his hit song, "Mother-in-Law." Sound familiar?

NAIL HER HEART WIDE OPEN

This simple spell is reputed to make your mother-in-law love you. All it takes are some steel nerves and fresh fingernail clippings.

1. Surprise your spouse by inviting his or her parents over for a meal.
2. Prior to the meal, in private, trim your fingernails, reserving the nail parings.
3. Using a mortar and pestle, grind or pound the nail parings until they are pulverized and powdery. (If you don't have a mortar and pestle, carefully wrap the parings inside a paper towel and smash them with a small hammer.)

Reserve the powdered parings in a safe, secret place for later use.
4. Prepare a nice meal, something that will please your mother-in-law. Maintain a reasonably serene, pleasant atmosphere throughout dinner.
5. Following the meal, excuse yourself to make coffee. Alone.
6. Add the nail-paring powder to your mother-in-law's cup.

Results should be apparent fairly quickly. If the spell starts to wear off, repeat it. Worst-case scenario? You at least have the personal satisfaction of knowing exactly what she drank.

ELIMINATION FUMIGATION

Oregano is alleged to keep troublesome in-laws at a distance. Greek oregano is reputedly the most potent.
1. First, tastefully arrange some photographs of your in-laws.
2. Grind the oregano into a fine powder, sprinkle it onto a small charcoal, and then burn the charcoal, wafting the smoke

towards the photos with a fan or feather.
3. Fumigate your home with oregano smoke, especially near doors and windows.
4. Alternatively, hang fresh oregano to dry in a cool, dark corner, away from direct sunlight. When dry, burn it as a smudge wand.

***

get your divorce

It's over! There's no going back. So why won't your spouse cooperate? Use some magical persuasion to make him see the light.

TEN STEPS TOWARD FREEDOM

1. You need appropriate male- and female-figure candles to represent you and your soon-to-be ex.
2. Carve your name and birthday into your candle, and your spouse's name and birthday into

the other one. Carve your wedding date into both candles and then cross that date out until it's illegible.
3. Dress the candles with *Command and Compel Oil.*
4. Stand the candles back to back.
5. Write your names, birthdays, and the wedding date on a piece of brown paper. Cross the wedding date out.
6. Cover his name on the paper by writing your own name over his, announcing "I cross you, I command you!"
7. Light the candle and burn it for fifteen minutes for seven consecutive days, each day pushing the candles a little farther apart from each other.
8. Each day, scorch the paper a little in the candle's flame, saying, "I command you, I compel you to divorce me. Give me my freedom now!"
9. During the seven-day period, you must quietly but firmly tell him or her of your wish for a divorce.

10. On the eighth day, burn the paper and candles completely.

THE BITTER END

Wormwood's reputation as the epitome of bitterness goes back to biblical times. So does its reputation for profound magical power. Use the essential oil to end a period of bitterness and move toward sweetness.

- If your "better half" still lives with you, add a few drops of the essential oil to the rinse water when you wash his or her clothes. Alternatively, sprinkle a few drops on his or her shoes and socks.
- If you no longer have access to clothing, write a letter and scent the paper and envelope with wormwood. The letter can be about anything; what is crucial is that you bring your no-longer-dearly-beloved into physical contact with the wormwood. He or she should soon become more receptive to the concept of divorce.
- Important! Do not use essential oil of wormwood in any other way. It

is extremely toxic and potentially fatal if ingested.

***

adjust the marital balance of power

Once upon a time, back in the early days of your relationship, you fell into a pattern, but it's becoming desperately urgent that the rules be changed!

FOLLOW ME, BOY!

The target of the spell must be male. This famous old formula allegedly makes a man take direction from the one who's wearing it. It also has a somewhat erotic component: if all goes as planned, he should obey with a smile!

1. Grind equal parts of catnip, damiana, and sweet flag (calamus) together with a mortar and pestle, working them to as fine a powder as possible.
2. Add the powder to a small vial of sweet almond oil.

- Wear this fragrant oil as a perfume. Offer to give him a massage and use this oil. Repeat as needed.
- For extra pacification, add a few drops of essential oil of patchouli to the blend.

MISTRESS OF THE HOUSE

Enough is enough! Be the mistress of your own home. This spell is sterner than the previous one. The initiator of the spell, the one who wishes to reap the benefits, must be female.

1. Grind dried sweet flag (calamus) root with a mortar and pestle while focusing on your desire. (Pretend it's his head or his pride that you're grinding, if that gives you any satisfaction.)
2. Add a tablespoon of the powdered sweet flag to a jar containing an ounce of sweet almond oil. Now add a devil's shoestring root, reputed to free you from the chains that bind you.

The roots will disperse their power and energy into the oil. Ideally you should massage his feet with the doctored oil (do *not* say what's in it or *why* you're offering the massage!) but if he won't go for it, just sprinkle a little oil on him or his shoes daily. This tactic is particularly effective if used while he's sleeping.

***

heal your broken heart

Friends tell you to get over it, but how can you move on when your world is filled with so much pain? Consider your broken heart a crisis that calls for healing and action rather than an eternal condition.

A SOLITARY LOVING CUP

This soothing potion applies balm to your broken heart and helps you contemplate a brand-new and happy future.

1. Steep balm of Gilead buds in red wine overnight.

2. Just before drinking the wine, add a few drops of either honeysuckle flower essence remedy (a Bach Flower Remedy) or boronia flower essence (an Australian Bush Flower Essence.)
3. Toast yourself at the first sighting of a new moon.
4. Repeat nightly until you feel much better.

HEARTBREAK BATH

More than just an excuse to pamper yourself (not that there's anything wrong with that!), this spell is comprised of flamed heart-healing components.
1. Blend a few drops of rose attar and essential oil of sandal-wood into a tablespoon of sweet almond oil and add to a full tub of warm water.
2. Sprinkle the bathwater with white rose petals and honeysuckle blossoms, if possible.
3. Light candles, dim the lights, and luxuriate in the water.

4. Repeat as needed.
Wear rose attar and a rose quartz crystal near your heart until your pain eases.

***

find your soul mate

*Got a moon above me,
But no one's here to love me,
Lover man, oh where can you be?*

Somewhere, your soul mate exists. What's taking him or her so long to show up? Here are some spells to hurry up the process.

ACE OF HEARTS LOVE SPELL

If you could make a person emerge from your dreams, who would it be?
1. From a deck of tarot cards, choose the knight, queen, or king who best exemplifes your ideal. (If another card suits you better—The Magician, let's say,

or The Empress—then use that one instead.)
2. Choose a figure candle (male or female) to represent your soul mate.
3. Dress the candle with essential oils of cinnamon and orange, fragrances sacred to Oshun, the Supreme Queen of Hearts.
4. Place the candle and a hand mirror before the upturned card.
5. On a piece of paper, list all the qualifications you require of your dream lover and your dream relationship, and anoint the corners of the page with the essential oils.
6. Place the paper beneath the candle.
7. Burn that candle, requesting that your true love find the path to your door as soon as possible. While the candle burns, spend some time gazing into the mirror, affirming that you deserve and are ready to receive what you wrote on the paper.

LA MADAMA'S DREAM POWDER

This classic formula allegedly turns romantic dreams into loving reality. Spicy and fragrant, there's no need to retire it once true love has arrived. This formula is also known as *Dreams of Delight Powder:* simmer some with red wine and serve it as an aphrodisiac, instead! Until that day, however, use it to attract true love:

1. Grind cardamom, cinnamon, coriander, and licorice root together, creating as fine a powder as possible.
2. Sprinkle the powder on charcoal and burn as incense.
3. Inhale the fumes and allow the scent to permeate your hair and clothes.

For added intensification, send a message to the Universe asking for what (or whom) you need. If you're at a loss for words, consistent repetitions of Billie Holiday's rendition

> of "Lover Man (Oh, Where Can You Be?)" works wonders!

***

get him back

You had him, but you lost him. Now you can't rest until he's back in your arms!

CLEOPATRA LOVE OIL

Cleopatra didn't take "no" for an answer. A superb linguist and an expert on beauty, snakes, and gynecology, it isn't clear what she knew about magic, but as she was considered to be the living presence of the goddess Isis on Earth, surely she knew something. Not that everything was smooth sailing for Cleopatra. She lost her beloved Marc Anthony for a while. He even married another. She got him back, though. He returned to her, ultimately dying in her arms.

1. Write your beloved's name on seven squares of yellow paper.

2. Anoint the corners with *Cleopatra Oil:* four drops of essential oil of cypress, three drops of essential oil of frankincense, four drops of essential oil of myrrh, and four drops of essential oil of neroli or petitgrain, all added to apricot kernel oil.
3. Carve your name and his together, surrounded by a heart, on each of seven pink votive candles and dress the candles with *Cleopatra Oil.*
4. Place one square of the anointed paper beneath each candle.
5. Beginning on a Friday, light and burn one candle a day.
6. After the third candle but before the last one has burned out, you must make some sort of overture to your lost love.

SWEET SUGAR MAGIC

Allegedly this powder will make him stop what he's doing and come on home.

1. Grind bay leaves, cinnamon, lavender, and star anise together

and then blend the resulting powder with an equal amount of powdered sugar.
2. If he left behind personal belongings, especially clothing, sprinkle the powder over them, ideally onto socks, underwear, or intimate apparel.
3. If he removed all his belongings (not a good sign, incidentally), then write a sweet, conciliatory love note, adding some of the sugar powder to the envelope before you seal it, and mail it to your beloved.

***

fit into your wedding dress

The dress is perfect! It can't be changed, so, unfortunately, if you want to wear it, you're the one who'll have to transform.

How I wish there was a potion that could miraculously remove those pounds overnight. Unfortunately, magical diets are like any others: the safe, healthy ones take a little time. Don't wait until the absolute last minute to start! These spells will reinforce, empower, and strengthen any other diet regimen.

For extra power, perform both spells in conjunction. They complement each other excellently.

CUT TO SIZE

1. Obtain a naked female figure candle.
2. Using a pin, scratch lines into the wax to show where reduction is needed, as you would were you taking in a dress. Dress the candle with *Reduction Oil* (essential oils of fennel, grapefruit and patchouli diluted in jojoba oil).
3. Burn the candle for fifteen minutes daily. After burning, use a craft knife to chip off wax and demonstrate your weight-loss plans and accomplishments. For instance, take a little more off the hips every day.

SKINNY DIP

1. Add four drops each of the essential oils of cypress, fennel, grapefruit, and patchouli to a warm bath. Climb in and inhale the fragrance.
2. Repeat this for seven nights.
3. Visualize yourself in your new shape while reaffirming vows to exercise and eat in a healthy, beneficial manner.

***

get pregnant

When the old-fashioned way isn't working...

WHAT A LITTLE MOONLIGHT CAN DO

1. Fill a bowl halfway with water, preferably ocean or river water, but bottled spring water will work, too.
2. Beginning at the new moon, take the bowl outside and leave it in

the moonlight for a minimum of three hours.
3. Carefully bring it inside and put the bowl of moon-charged water under the bed in the vicinity of where the woman's belly most frequently rests. For maximum effectiveness, the woman should attempt to keep her belly situated above the bowl as much as possible, whenever she's in the bed.
4. Repeat this ritual for fourteen nights or until the appearance of the full moon. Make love as inspired.

FILLED TO THE BRIM

1. Line a charm bag with some dried mother of thyme.
2. Fill the bag with cowrie shells, a small piece of silver, and a lodestone anointed with *Astarte Oil* (coriander, jasmine, neroli or petitgrain, and rose essential oils in sweet almond oil). Astarte is the ancient Semitic spirit of

fertility; her name is believed to mean "filled womb."
3. Wear the bag around your waist, under your clothes. (Anointing the woman's thighs with *Astarte Oil* prior to sex may also be beneficial.)

> Verify that all containers in your home (boxes, canisters, vases and so on) are not empty. Place tiny baby doll toys inside anything that could be construed as an empty container.

***

prevent miscarriage and premature delivery

Nine months can seem so long! So much time and opportunity for so much to go wrong!

HOLD TIGHT!

1. At the first sign of trouble, take a strong cord and tie one knot in it.

2. Strongly visualize the knot as your baby, focus on the strength of the knot and speak to your child: "As this knot holds firm, so you hold firm in my womb. Do not loosen from my hold until (the expected date of delivery)."
3. Place the cord in a secure container or wrap it firmly in a baby blanket. Keep it in a safe place until the time is right for delivery and then the knot must be released.

AMBERELLA'S BABY GUARDIAN

According to Baltic legend, Amberella was a princess who abandoned human life for immortality and true love under the waves as the bride of a Prince of the Sea. She occasionally has regrets, though, and when she does, she showers humans with treasures, amber in particular.

Amber is believed to ground and stabilize both the mother and her unborn child. It's traditionally worn around the waist for best effect.

If you have a string of amber beads long enough to span your belly, wear it. Otherwise, wrap a piece of amber and an angelica root in red cloth and wear it at your waist beneath your clothing. A red-flannel drawstring bag is perfect if one is at hand, but in a situation like this, where urgency is imperative, it's the color that's key. A red scarf or handkerchief or even a piece of red fabric torn from another garment will suit your purposes.

This should prevent you from stumbling and your baby from descending before the right time!

> Avoid wearing or carrying lodestones or emeralds, both of which are reputed to speed delivery.

***

turn a breech baby

Come on, baby, head down!

TURN THAT BABY AROUND!

For this spell, you need an image that represents your baby to you. Use a photograph, a drawing, or a baby doll.
1. Sit down facing the image.
2. Turn it upside down and talk to it.
3. Explain simply, as if to a child, why it's imperative that he or she turns upside down—and stays that way!
4. Repeatedly turn the image, rotating it in a slow, calm, clockwise motion from the upright position to upside-down. Repeat this several times daily.

FOLLOW ME, BABY

A trusted partner is needed for this spell. It may be a good opportunity to get baby's dad involved in your first family conference.
1. Lie down and let your partner gently massage your stomach with apricot kernel oil. (This is a fixed or true oil, an "oily" oil,

not an essential oil, most of which are unsafe for use during pregnancy.)
2. Locate the baby.
3. Gently rub a lodestone on your belly in clockwise circles to direct the baby to the proper position.
4. While the other person provides direction, you concentrate deeply on transmitting the concept of turning over to the baby, explaining why it's crucial and what he or she needs to do.

***

new-mother magic

Oh, the things they neglected to tell you...

INCREASE MOTHER'S MILK

If breast-feeding is so natural, why is it sometimes so frustrating? Well, for starters, modern cultural expectations aren't always in line with the most primal human skills, including magic and nursing.

Concerned about your milk supply? Turquoise is reputed to increase it. You'll need a chain of turquoise beads to wear around your neck, ideally one long enough to hang between your breasts.

1. Cover one teaspoon of fennel seeds with one cup of boiling water and let it steep for ten minutes. Uncrushed fennel seeds will create a sweeter tea; crush the seeds if you prefer a stronger, more bitter taste. Strain the fennel from the liquid and bring the tea into your bedroom. (Better yet: have someone else fix and bring it to you!)
2. Undress from the waist up, leaving on only your turquoise necklace and go to bed with Baby. Anyone who can't see you this way is just not allowed in the room.
3. Sip your tea, wear your necklace, hold your baby, and don't get out of bed for anything other than the absolute needs of nature. The baby should wear as

few clothes as possible, too, for maximum skin-to-skin contact.
4. Let your baby nurse on demand.

If obtaining the necklace is not feasible, then just fix the tea and follow the other steps of the spell. The two components of the spell (the tea and the turquoise), however, do greatly complement each other.

DECREASE COLIC

Colic is a mysterious ailment that defies definition and control. What is certain is that it sure makes a baby cranky and drives you crazy! Fennel seeds are an ancient remedy. As they're used for the nursing spell as well, it's obvious why fennel can be a new mother's best friend. Use dried seeds—*never* the essential oil—for both spells.

1. Add one-half teaspoon of fennel seeds to one cup of just-boiled spring water.

2. Let it steep for ten minutes. Strain out the seeds and allow the liquid to cool.
3. Gently feed one tablespoon of the fennel water to the baby. If fennel doesn't work, weak infusions of dill or caraway seeds may also be effective. Do not combine the herbs, however; create an infusion from only one botanical at a time.

***

help me make it through the night

You gave birth to new life, but now you've transformed into a zombie, one of the walking dead. Sleep deprivation is a certified form of torture. Use these magic tools to get a good night's sleep.

MAMA'S SLEEPY-TIME MASSAGE OIL

1. Blend two drops each of German chamomile, petitgrain, and

sandalwood essential oils into a tablespoon of apricot kernel oil.
2. Before bedtime, apply the oil to your face gently with upward strokes. (Added bonus: these oils benefit the complexion.)
3. Take the baby to bed with you. Don't apply the oils to the baby, but instead allow him or her to inhale the fragrance on your body. If baby falls asleep, go to sleep too. Don't worry about getting the baby out of your bed, just fall asleep as quickly as you can and forbid anyone but the baby from awakening you!

BABY'S SWEET SLUMBER PILLOW

Make your baby a dream pillow containing dried hops, vervain, and chamomile blossoms. Sew the botanicals into a little bag and then put that inside a second bag made of the softest possible flannel in white or pale blue. If you're too exhausted for sewing, just stuff the herbs into a drawstring bag.

Either way, hang it close enough to the baby for the fragrance to waft over him or her, but far enough away to be out of reach. Older children who've graduated from the oral stage may sleep with their pillow.

***

protect a child

The most intense period of psychic danger is traditionally believed to be during infancy: the first eight days of life for a boy and the first twenty-one for a girl. Most traditional cultures keep kids well stocked with amulets and spiritual guards until maturity is well within sight.

NO DANGER PERMITTED IN THE RED ZONE

Here's a simple and ancient Jewish spell: Tie a red thread or ribbon around Baby's cradle or bed. That's it, sufficient to ward off dangers.

ANCIENT EGYPTIAN CHILD CARE

On the other hand, perhaps a more complex ritual would heighten your sense of security? The ancient Egyptians, who possessed a particularly family-oriented culture, put a lot of effort into devising ways to protect their children from the world's dangers, both physical and spiritual. Egyptian spirits are especially vigilant and practiced guardians of children.

1. Obtain a statue of each of the following deities: Isis, Bes, Taweret, and Bastet. All are extremely devoted to children and are potentially fierce protectors.
2. Place one statue in each corner of the child's bedroom, each turned to face the bed.
3. Activate the statues by burning frankincense and myrrh resin in the room: smudge each statue with the smoke.
4. Stand in the center of the room and clearly explain to each spirit,

as represented by their statues, its mission of protection. If necessary, repeat the same invocation four times.
5. Burn frankincense and myrrh weekly, or whenever you perceive that they have worked on your behalf, so as to revive their power.

***

find trustworthy child care

Do you remember the effectiveness of the children's advertisement for a nanny in the movie Mary Poppins? Well, where is Mary Poppins when you need her?

NANNY NEEDED NOW!

This spell does not exclusively provide nannies but will serve to help locate any type of dependable child care. Use this spell to find the child care that is most appropriate for your needs.
1. Set a table that would make a proper British nanny proud.

2. Using your best china (buy a fancy paper plate if necessary), brew a fresh pot of fine tea (looseleaf, not bags, if you please!) and serve it on a white lace doily alongside a plate of crumpets or scones with cream.
3. Seat yourself at the table and write a letter explaining, in detail, everything you need from a child care provider.
4. Carve a white cat candle with the names and birthdays of you and your children. Place the letter under the candle, then burn the candle.

SWAMP ISIS TRUSTED CHILD CARE AGENCY

Isis, the Great Goddess and Mistress of Magic, She of One-Thousand Names, wasn't always all-powerful. Once upon a time, she was a broke single mother forced to labor long hours to support her child and lacking adequate childcare. That lack of adequate supervision almost resulted in the death of her beloved only son. Only Isis' supreme magical skills saved him, but then *she's* a goddess. Ask her for assistance.

1. You will need a statue of Isis. You may also use a blue candle to represent her.
2. Surround the candle with toy crocodiles, the creatures who embody fierce, devoted, protective motherhood. (Crocodiles don't need child care; they carry their babies in their mouths. Who's going to tell *them* to leave the kids at home?)
3. Add six drops each of essential oil of myrrh and rose attar to a small spray bottle containing spring water.
4. Disperse the mist into the air to call Isis.
5. Speak to her from your heart and tell her exactly what you need. Promise her that, should her assistance be forthcoming, as soon as you are able, you will act as her representative on Earth and help another person in need.

***

make your children behave in public

Presumably you've already tried good old bribery and blackmail.

HOUSE OF SWEETNESS AND CHARM

Maybe there was a reason why Hansel and Gretel were sent out into the woods?

1. Begin constructing a Hansel and Gretel house, complete with witch, children, and candy. The house itself may be made from gingerbread or a box.
2. Do this in the presence of your little ones, but do not explain what you're doing. Work as silently as possible. You will capture their attention. They may watch you work, but they cannot participate. If their nagging really strains your nerves—try hard to hold out—allow them to hand you things, but not to actually touch the house.

3. Work on the house for fifteen to thirty minutes daily. It will not have the desired effect if it's completed in one sitting.
4. If the house is knocked down, ruined, or wrecked at any time, just start again.
5. Include as much detail as possible, adding lots of candy. The candy can stay wrapped, though, and does not have to be eaten. There's no need for a sugar rush!
6. You may allow your creative expression to have free reign. The only requirements are these: each of your children, whether personally incorrigible or not, must be represented by a specific child figure. The witch must also have a tiny working cauldron; if you can't find a miniature cauldron, a metal thimble will do.
7. When the house is complete, burn anise seeds and lavender blossoms in the cauldron.

This spell will insidiously implant some sweetness and patience into your little vagabonds!

GOOD BEHAVIOR POTION

Direct descendants of alchemists' potions, flower essence remedies are pure water charged with the aura and power of specific plants. Safe enough to be used by children, they exert a profound effect upon the personality and psyche. Use them to initiate some behavioral adjustments.

1. Blend together five drops each of chicory, crab apple, and vine flower essence remedies (Bach Flowers).
2. Add this blend to your child's nightly bath or, if he or she will let you, use the blend to give the child a foot massage. This latter method is particularly effective.

***

stop a bully

There are two approaches to this dilemma: either co-opt the bully or invoke a bigger one.

THE SHIELD OF THE FLAMING SWORD

This spell petitions the Archangel Michael to erect a shield around you and keep you within the arms of safety!

1. Burn frankincense and myrrh to attract Michael's attention.
2. Call him with this invocation:
   Michael to the right of me, Michael to the left of me,
   Michael above me, Michael below me,
   Michael within me, Michael all around me,
   Michael with your flaming sword of cobalt blue,
   Protect me today!

3. Describe your situation to him. Request his assistance. (The potential assistance offered by a guardian angel is exponentially

magnified when that help is directly requested.)
4. Place an angelica root inside a white or gold drawstring pouch together with a miniature sword (a fancy toothpick also works).
5. Anoint the pouch with frankincense and myrrh and carry it with you.

> Michael's invocation can be repeated daily or as frequently as needed.

SUGAR SWEET

If you can't beat 'em, maybe they can learn to love you.
1. Carve your tormentor's name into a brown candle three times, beginning at the bottom of the candle and working your way up.
2. Place the candle in a bowl filled with brown sugar.
3. Focus on your desire and light the candle, letting it burn for approximately thirty minutes.

4. Repeat the wish-and-burn sequence for nine nights before allowing the candle to completely burn out.
5. Finally, collect any remaining wax and sugar and wrap them in plastic. Traditionally, this spell is considered most effective if you dispose of the remains by leaving the packet in your enemy's path or in his or her yard or property. However, there's no need to get yourself into worse trouble. Disposing of the remains in a garbage can in the vicinity of your enemy will be effective, too.

***

lose your daughter's evil boyfriend

These spells verge on malevolent magic, so make sure your intentions are true. Evil is the key word: you can't just break up a couple because you don't like his looks. If you're pretty sure you recognize his face from the post-office wall, however, don't hesitate to act!

BREAK UP, AND NO MAKING UP!

This very ancient spell from Western Asia was easier to accomplish in the days before indoor plumbing, back in the days when you actually knew the hen whose eggs you ate. If you're willing to take the trouble, however, this spell can still be accomplished.

1. Obtain an egg laid by a black hen.
2. Hard-boil it in urine, either his, hers, or yours.
3. Peel the egg and feed half to a cat and the other half to a dog, saying, "Just the way you two are natural enemies, so shall (his name) and (her name) feel about each other."

This spell subscribes to the retro notion that cats and dogs can't get along. Play along if you want the spell to work. Don't feed the egg to your own pet cat and dog who adore each other. Instead, find a cat and dog who aren't enthralled with the other species.

ONE POTATO, TWO POTATO

When she needs the right boyfriend, you need the right potato.

1. Search for a potato that's half-rotten, but still good on the other side. Cut it in half.
2. Toss the rotten half in the gutter, away from your home. If it's rained lately and the gutter's full of rapidly running water, all the better. So much for the bad half!
3. Now, take the good half and make a potato stamp by carving away the outer surface so a heart shape stands in relief.
4. Stamp hearts on cards using gold and red inks so that they resemble valentines, and then use them to decorate a *Happy, Healthy Love* altar dedicated to your daughter. Make a list of all the wonderful things you wish for her, place it under a pink candle and burn!

***

end sibling rivalry

Are they driving you crazy? Are they transforming your home into hell? Nip that rivalry in the bud!

PEACE IN THE FAMILY

Do they have you so frazzled that you'd love to send them on a dragon quest? They'd either have to learn to be loving partners or else never come back to bother you. Dragon's Blood is a red resin from Indonesia. Use it to calm any domestic disturbance.

1. Pulverize Dragon's Blood resin with sugar and salt using a mortar and pestle.
2. Put the powder in a matchbox and put the matchbox in a white envelope.
3. Seal the envelope and hide it. As long as no one discovers it, you should have peace.

You can also try placing a round crystal ball at the foot of each bed in your home. This feng shui tip is reputed to eliminate sibling rivalry and encourage familial harmony and good relations!

WHITE ROSE OF LOVE AND FRIENDSHIP

1. Gently mix two parts white rose petals with one part cumin seed.
2. Add one tablespoon of this botanical mixture to one ounce of extra-virgin olive oil.
3. Add this to a spray bottle of spring water. Shake the bottle vigorously and disperse the spray throughout the home, particularly in areas where the rivalry is strongest. If your spray bottle gets clogged or you prefer an atmospheric approach, a white rose may be used to disperse the soothing potion. Just dip the rose into the spring-water concoction and sprinkle gently.

section three

home

Shelter ranks among the most basic human needs, right behind oxygen, food, and drink. Emergencies in matters of housing spell true crisis.

general principles

• The archangel Michael is humanity's staunch defender. Call him when you need his flaming sword of defense.

• It was Michael who first demonstrated the use of angelica root to ward off plague and disaster. It is still used as a personal protective device.

• The numbers five, seven, and nine best radiate protection. Three, ten, and twelve radiate happiness and fulfillment.

• The color black epitomizes protection and safety, while lodestones draw your deepest desires toward you.

find a home

Let's start with a basic need: a roof over your head!

BUILD YOUR DREAM HOUSE

1. With the open end on top, turn a cardboard box into a model of your dream home using crayons and other art supplies. In order to give the magic a shot at working, keep your model home reasonably realistic. In other words, don't create a medieval castle or anything too unlikely to ever materialize! Make it a home that could at least theoretically be yours. Decorate the box with as much detail as possible.
2. Prepare a candle by carving your name and birthday into the wax. Dress it with *Lucky Lodestone Oil*.
3. On a piece of brown paper, write a letter to Earth. Tell her exactly what you need, what you would like, and what you can afford.

Be as specific as possible: if you need northern lightning and a bus stop no more than two blocks away, write that down.

4. Place the letter inside the box and put the candle on top of the letter.
5. Sprinkle magnetic sand into a dish of honey and smear this on the inner walls of your "house."
6. Light your candle. Keep the candle supervised at all times—it's extremely inauspicious to burn down your house. Visualize yourself in your home, safe, secure, and happy. Extinguish the flame whenever it becomes necessary and consider your spell complete.

HOME SEARCH

1. Get the real estate listings from a newspaper or flyer.
2. Using red ink, circle any ads for appropriate housing. They don't have to be exactly what you're looking for, just in the right ballpark.

3. Only one page is required for this spell. At the top of the page, write your name and birthday, the present date, the day by which you need your new home, and the preferred price and location.
4. Dab the corners of the paper with *Lucky Lodestone Oil.*
5. Fold the page over twice to form a squarish shape. Keep it under your pillow or mattress until your request is fulfilled.
6. Begin searching in earnest for your new abode.

***

keep your home: prevent eviction

The thought of being forced from your home ranks among the scariest of all fears.
- *The first spell works on your landlord's congeniality, encouraging cooperation and generosity.*
- *The second helps plant you in your home like a sturdy tree.*

LANDLORD FIX!

Should this spell bring you success, reinforce it annually by giving your landlord a full-size bottle of liquor at the winter holidays.

1. Write your landlord's name nine times on a square of brown paper.
2. Put the paper in an empty plastic soda bottle together with one shot each of gin, rum, vodka, and whiskey.
3. Add two tablespoons of sugar. The traditional spell now directs you to add one tablespoon each of river water, well water, and cistern water; however, I appreciate that this may be unrealistic in these modern times. Substitute spring water for the river water and mineral water for the well water. If you can get water straight from a rain gutter to substitute for the cistern water, that's ideal. If not, just use plain rainwater.
4. Cap the bottle and place it upside down in a corner behind

your bed or in a deep corner of your closet. Reinforce the spell as necessary by shaking the bottle at either noon or midnight.

GROUNDED LIKE A ROCK

So effective that it may foil your own plans to move, skip this spell if you're only trying to stay put long enough to find another home.

You'll need one piece of charcoal, one rock (preferably from your property), and some benzoin, an Asian resin burned to establish sacred space, plus a metal grater and a mortar and pestle.

1. Grate a little bit of the rock and charcoal into the mortar. Grind them together with the pestle.
2. Add a little bit of the benzoin and mash it together with the charcoal and rock dust.
3. Scatter the mixture across the front threshold of your home and any other ports of entry (doors, large windows—any-place where someone could conceivably enter

your home). Scatter protective boundaries as needed.
4. Repeat this procedure whenever the threat reappears. Use the same charcoal and rock. If you run out of charcoal, it may be replaced. If the threat isn't over by the time the rock is gone, however, it's time to consider moving on. To avoid that situation, choose a large rock.

***

home protection spells

Your home is your castle. Maintain it as a strong, well-protected fortress.

FIERY WALL OF PROTECTION

This classic condition oil evokes the protection of the archangel Michael. You'll find the basic formula (in section entitled "A Formulary of Condition Oils"). When using the oil, visualize Michael's flaming sword glowing cobalt blue as a shield around your home.

- Sprinkle the oil around your home, concentrating on doors, windows, and any other spots you consider vulnerable.
- You may also add the oil to a spray bottle of spring water. Shake vigorously, then spray all the corners of your home and depths of your closets.

SPECIAL HOME PROTECTION CHARM

This talisman produces a protective aura that reinforces any more conventional techniques that you use to protect yourself and your home.

1. Combine dried five-ginger grass and gardenia petals.
2. Sprinkle the herbs with five drops of essential oil of sandalwood.
3. Allow the essential oil to dry completely before placing the herbs inside a small red-flannel drawstring pouch.
4. Add an angelica root and a pinch of salt. Place the charm discreetly inside a cabinet near

your front door, preferably facing it.

***

sell your home fast

You needed to unload that property yesterday!

SAINT JOSEPH, UNLOAD MY HOME!

Invoke Saint Joseph, the patron of stepfathers and homeowners, to sell your home on the double.

1. In your backyard, bury a small statue of St. Joseph head down and facing away from your home.
2. Petition him to help you sell your home fast.

Bribery works with saints and spirits, too! Tell him what you'll do for him if the home is sold within a specific period of time. (Charitable donations and efforts work best!)

UP IN SMOKE!

Joss paper (Chinese wishing paper) is available in the Chinatown markets of many cities, as well as from feng shui supply outlets. It's believed that, when burned, this paper promptly transmits your messages to the appropriate spirit power, sort of like the message-carrying owls in the Harry Potter novels who always know where to deliver the mail.

1. Write your needs on a piece of joss paper as specifically and lucidly as you can.
2. Place one drop of lotus oil in the center of the page. Anoint the corners with essential oils of cinnamon and sandalwood.
3. Burn the paper. Do not leave it unattended, stay with it, focusing on your desires, petitioning and praying until every last letter has gone up in smoke. (Make sure that every last bit of the paper burns, especially those bits containing writing.)

***

buy your dream home without going broke

The house is perfect—it's exactly what you need! Unfortunately, the price is well beyond your reach.

For these spells to work, carefully consider what is realistic for you and be willing to give your seller your best offer.

SOFTEN UP AND TAKE MY OFFER

1. Dress a purple candle with good old *Command and Compel Oil*.
2. Write the seller's name, as well as that of his or her attorney, realtor, and anyone else involved in the deal, nine times each onto parchment.
3. Cover each name by writing your own over it, saying aloud, "I command you, I compel you to accept my price."
4. Place the paper under the candle.

5. State your wish. (Traditionally, for best results, the Twenty-third Psalm is now recited.)
6. Burn the candle.

A HANDSHAKE DEAL

1. Add red brick dust and ground deer's tongue (the herb) to a jar filled with a half-cup of olive oil.
2. Add nine drops of essential oil of patchouli.
3. Add a lodestone. Close the jar, shake it and let it sit overnight.
4. Rub some of the oil into your palms and make sure to touch the seller's hands during negotiations, while simultaneously mentally focusing on your goal.

***

find tenants

Unloading the property isn't your problem. What you'd like to do is fill the hollow space with tenants. Both these spells adjust your property's aura and may be used to attract residential or business tenants.

A FRAGRANT LURE

Use the dried components of *Van Van Oil* to keep your property occupied.

1. Combine chopped dried lemongrass and vetiver. It's difficult to find the other Asian grasses, but if you can get them, add them!
2. Add hyssop, lavender blossoms, sandalwood powder, and spearmint and grind everything as finely as possible.
3. Sprinkle the dust on charcoal and burn it as incense. Walk the smoke through the property, beginning at the front door.

FILL ME UP NOW!

1. Insert a lodestone and a High John the Conqueror root into a vial of *Van Van Oil*. Allow them to soak overnight, preferably in the moonlight.
2. Anoint a small magnetic horseshoe with the oil. Hang it over the building's front door. (A

real horseshoe may be substituted for a magnetic one.)

***

make your neighbors move

Your block isn't big enough for both of you. Although they have driven you to consider it, leaving really isn't an option for you right now. The only alternative is for them to move.

MAGIC MOVING VAN

1. Write the offending neighbors' names on each knob of a black seven-knob candle.
2. Anoint the candle with *Banishing Oil* and Tabasco® brand pepper sauce.[4] Wash your hands *well*

---

[4] The reason to use Tabasco® sauce, as opposed to other brands, is that it contains only three ingredients: salt and vinegar (which are protective and purifying) and hot peppers (which are a key component of banishing formulas). If you do use another brand, make sure it contains no sugar or other sweetening

immediately after this step. Do not touch your eyes or any sensitive parts of the body until you do!
3. Beginning at the full moon, burn one knob a night.

TOSS 'EM OUT WITH THE COFFEE GROUNDS

1. Combine cayenne pepper, used coffee grounds, and dirt collected from your neighbors' footsteps or from beneath a chair in which they've sat. If more than one neighbor is involved, target the one who annoys you most or the one you perceive as being the decision maker.
2. Add ground sassafras powder (herb shops call it ground sassafras; your supermarket calls it filé powder and displays it with the Cajun spices).
3. Discreetly sprinkle the powder on your neighbors' doorstep

agents, which could potentially neutralize this spell.

while strongly visualizing their house vacant and surrounded by a happy neighborhood!

***

make undesirable houseguests leave

Your house is not a hotel. The party's over. It's been over for you for a while. Starting to have doubts as to whether they'll ever leave? They're not taking your hints—or maybe you're not in a position to drop any.

EXODUS NOW!

They've stayed so long, surely their stuff has accumulated around the house. Pick up a few items, ones as intimate as possible. (Offer to do their laundry, if you aren't doing it already.) What's the worst-case scenario? If things go missing, maybe they'll leave.

1. Construct a small doll using these personal items. If more than one guest is involved,

create an individual doll for each person.
2. Try to make the dolls identifiable, but just in case the spirit message isn't clear enough, write your guests' names on small slips of brown paper. Cover the names by writing "Leave my home now!" over them until the names are illegible. Pin the nametags to the front of each doll.
3. Whip up either some *Banishing Oil* or *Exodus Oil.* For the latter, combine one-half teaspoon each of asafetida, cayenne pepper, and sulfur powder. Add that to an ounce of castor oil. Shake vigorously.
4. Soak the doll's feet with the oil. Keep the doll in a safe, discreet place. Rub oil on the feet daily, while silently telling your guests everything you'd love to say out loud. Conclude by mentally ordering your visitor(s) to *get out now!*

Once the guests are gone, there's no need to keep the doll as a souvenir of the good times. Remove the doll or dolls from your home as soon as possible. Drop them in a garbage can as far away from your home as possible, arriving at and leaving the garbage can via as circuitous a route as possible.

RUN LIKE A THIEF

This spell is attributed to the great Voodoo priestess, Marie Laveau.

1. Write each of your guests' names nine times on a piece of brown paper. Cover and cross out each name by writing your own name over it.
2. Place the paper in a small glass jar or bottle, then fill that with *Four Thieves Vinegar.*
3. Seal the container tightly.
4. The traditional mode of disposal is to throw the bottle over your left shoulder into running water, without looking back, but you may also dispose of it in a garbage can as far as possible from your home, which you will arrive at and depart from via a

circuitous route. Remember: Don't look back!

***

banish ghosts

A ghost in the house can sometimes be an asset, adding some haunting ambience to your home's atmosphere, while offering advice from the other side and plenty of fuel for conversation. However, even ghosts need to maintain good behavior. Perhaps your ghost lacks the manners of a good houseguest. Learning to coexist with a ghost is probably easier than ghost busting but if yours is giving you a hard time, try these ancient and effective remedies.

JUNO'S BREW

Juno, Spirit Queen of ancient Rome, the deified Mistress of the House, is a fierce defender of the hearth. She doesn't appreciate unwelcome guests. The floor wash named in her honor is reputed to force out spirits and malign forces.

1. Place one-half cup of vervain in a bowl and cover it with boiling water.
2. Let it steep for ten minutes, then strain and add the liquid and some white vinegar to a bucket of water.
3. Wash your floors, beginning at the center of each room, then working your way to the corners and out the front door, all the while sending mental *"Get out!"* messages to your unwanted guest.
4. When you've finished, leave all the doors and windows wide open for thirty minutes.

GO TO THE DEVIL!

The spice asafetida is little known in Western countries, except as a component of Worcestershire sauce. It's a popular ingredient in Indian cuisine, however, and is easily purchased in Indian groceries or stores catering to gourmet cooks. Also known as devil's dirt, when burned its pungent aroma allegedly creates an exorcising effect, driving evil spirits far away. The smell is genuinely awful; you'll want to leave home, too.

To prevent you from packing your bags, burn asafetida together with frankincense and myrrh, which smell beautiful and will summon strong, righteous spirits to protect your home.

In North Africa, asafetida is burned and the smoke is wafted around people bearing the marks of possession. It's also alleged to soothe panic attacks and protect against psychically derived illnesses.

***

pest control

You're playing host to the worst guests of all: Bugs. They've made themselves comfortably at home and seem to have no intention of ever leaving.

MY AIM IS TRUE

Ochossi is West Africa's divine hunter: When he aims his arrows, the prey *never* escapes. Ask him for

assistance in eradicating pests from your home.
1. Add cornmeal and honey to a glass of milk and stir gently to blend.
2. Petition Ochossi to trap and/or remove the creatures that plague you.
3. Leave the offering of milk in full view for at least several hours, if not longer.

This spell is particularly beneficial should you wish to avoid chemical pesticides. Ochossi is also a guardian of the woodlands and a botanical expert: He prefers traditional hunting methods. You may accompany this spell with mousetraps, roach motels, or similar methods, if you choose. Allow Ochossi to guide your hands and your intuition.

A VISIT TO THE QUEEN

Perhaps the bugs themselves aren't your only problem: Maybe you philosophically oppose extermination and your conscience would rest easier if the little critters had a chance to get away.

The following spell may resolve those dilemmas. Be sure that you are in a calm, secure state of mind before proceeding with this visualization.

1. You must pay a visit to the spiritual queen of whatever species plagues you, for instance, the Ant Queen or the Cockroach Queen. Steel your nerves and take some deep breaths.
2. Visualize yourself journeying to her palace. It will be in the form of the creature's natural habitation, so the Ant Queen resides in an anthill, while the Wasp Queen lives in a nest. You and the queen must be of comparable size throughout the visualization.
3. Enter her domain. You will be met by courtiers and guards. Calmly but firmly emphasize that you have urgent confdential business to discuss with the queen and only with the queen.
4. When you are in her presence, be respectful but firm. Explain that her creatures can no longer

share your home. Clearly demarcate your territory, if necessary. Be as polite as if she were the Queen of England but also make it clear that you are a formidable adversary, not to be trifed with.

5. Give her a deadline for complete withdrawal of her subjects, allowing a generous but realistic (for you) amount of time. Explain that if the deadline is not met, steps may be taken to eradicate them from your home.

6. If your journey is a mission of mercy, an attempt to save the creatures from an extermination process that you do not desire and have not ordered, let the Queen know this. In that case, you may ask her to give you a gift before you depart. If you are offering an ultimatum of your own volition, however, do not ask for anything.

7. When your message has been delivered and your conversation is complete, respectfully bid

good-bye to the queen and retrace your journey.

section four

trouble

> Romance, careers, money—some emergencies can be neatly categorized. Unfortunately, life also produces a seemingly endless variety of crises and catastrophes with only one thing in common: They're all trouble!
>
> ***general principles***
> • Three, five, and seven are the most powerful numbers of protection.
> • The color blue wards off trouble and soothes frazzled nerves.
> • The most potent and helpful spirits are your personal allies and guardian angels. However, Kwan Yin, Goddess of Mercy, has vowed to come to the aid of anyone who cries out her name in desperation.

quit smoking

Legal, affordable, available, many people find smoking to be among the hardest addictions to break. Too bad you've just discovered that the thirteen-hour flight you have to take is completely non-smoking.

GRAPEFRUIT RELIEF

All you need for this spell is grapefruit; the quantity depends upon the intensity of your cravings. Metaphysically, grapefruit serves as an antidote to addiction. Possessing a strong cleansing effect, this fruit born in the Western Hemisphere is particularly effective for breaking the shackles of tobacco, an addiction born in the Americas.

1. Whenever you crave a cigarette, reach for a grapefruit instead.
2. Here's the catch: For the spell to work, your grapefruit cannot be cut with a knife or eaten with a spoon. Peel the fruit by hand. (If the peel is very tough, you may make the initial cut with a knife, but then continue by hand only.)
3. Separate the fruit into segments and eat them one by one,

chewing thoroughly and sucking out the juice.
4. Repeat as needed.

HERBAL HELPER

You'll need a blue candle, a candle-carving tool, and approximately one teaspoon each of dried anise seeds, ground cinnamon (or one small stick), cloves, sage, and St. John's Wort. Time your spell to coincide with the waning moon.

1. Hold the unlit candle in both hands and visualize yourself free of the habit you wish to break. Affirm: "I control my desires."
2. Beginning at the top of the candle and working your way down, carve your name and birthday into the wax.
3. At the base of the candle, carve the current date and then carve a tiny cigarette into the wax. Scratch an x over the cigarette.
4. Concentrate on your wish and affirmation once more and then light the candle.

5. While the candle is burning, use a mortar and pestle to vigorously grind the dried herbs together. Allow the motion to release any anger and frustration.
6. Place the herbs in a small pouch and carry it with you at all times, placing it beneath your pillow or beside your bed when you sleep.
7. Should you experience intense cravings, open the bag and inhale the herbs.
8. Repeat as frequently as needed.

> Indulge in a full-body massage incorporating the fragrant essential oil immortelle, also known as helichrysum, reputed to speed detoxification and hasten the departure of aches and cravings.

***

gag the gossips

Slander, gossip, rumors, and false accusations: Ruining a reputation or killing a good name can be tantamount to murder. Protect yourself.

GOSSIP PATROL

Based on Turkish tradition, this spell involves group effort. It combines a request for spiritual protection with a divination ritual to help determine the most effective manner to combat the situation. In addition to the participation of the victims, at least two people (preferably more) are needed to serve as ritual assistants. Make sure they are completely sympathetic to your cause.

1. First, the victim or victims of the gossip must be prepared with prayers. Have the victim(s) sit in the center of the room with their assistants surrounding them. Pray, petition, make spiritual requests and invocations as deemed appropriate.
2. Carefully melt wax in a double boiler.
3. While the victim of the gossip remains seated, someone else must hold a white cloth over his or her head. If the gossip

concerns more than one person, using a white tablecloth may be best.
4. Hold a small bowl of ice-cold water above the cloth.
5. Pour a small quantity of hot, melted wax into the water. As the wax hits the water, it should harden and form shapes.
6. Remove the shapes from the water once they've cooled. The victim or victims, together with their ritual assistants, can then study the shapes, which when analyzed and interpreted may offer advice and insight into the situation.
7. Once the shapes have been analyzed, dispose of them in a river or other natural waterway.

> Absolute worst-case scenario? Those wagging tongues won't be stilled? *Crown of Success Oil* won't stop gossip, but it will prevent it from adversely affecting you. Add it to your bath water and hold your head high!

FIERY WALL OF REPUTATION REPAIR

Fiery Wall of Protection Oil stifles vicious gossip. You'll find the formula in (section entitled "A Formulary of Condition Oils".

1. Carve your name, birthday, and any other pertinent information into a black cat candle.
2. Dress the candle with *Fiery Wall of Protection Oil and burn it!*

For extra action:
- Add *Fiery Wall of Protection Oil* to your bath.
- Put some in a spray bottle filled with spring water. Spray the mist into the air in front of you and then step into its protective veil.
- Drip a little oil onto some slippery elm herb and carry it with you in a red-flannel drawstring bag.

***

make a liar confess

You need the truth! You know you're being lied to, but you can't prove it. Or maybe you can't quite put your finger on the lie. Exert some magical pressure and pin the perpetrator down!

LIAR, COME CLEAN!

1. Dress a large purple candle with *Command and Compel Oil.*
2. Write your suspect's name nine times on brown paper.
3. Write your own name over each of the nine names.
4. Place the paper under the candle.
5. The candle will be burned in increments for seven consecutive nights.
6. When you light the candle each night, call out the person's name and say, "I command you, I compel you to tell me the truth."
7. Let the candle burn all the way on the final night.
8. After the seven nights are over, wrap any leftover wax in butcher's paper and dispose of it far from your home.

THIEF, COME CLEAN!

Something belonging to you has been stolen. You're not sure who took it and the denials aren't ringing true. This spell helps to expose a thief.

1. Using a mortar and pestle, grind together equal quantities of galangal root, vetiver, pokeroot, and hydrangea blossoms.
2. Sprinkle the powder at the place where the item was stolen or where it was last seen. The thief's identity should become known to you shortly.

***

speed your path to a green card

Use these rituals to provide protection from the immigration service, prevent deportation, and enable you to live freely and in peace wherever you want.

LAW, KEEP AWAY!

1. Place a High John the Conqueror root, a galangal root, a teaspoon of asafetida powder and a tablespoon of dried hydrangea blossoms in a jar.
2. Add enough olive oil to cover the contents. Allow them to soak overnight in the light of a full moon.
3. Strain the solids from the oil. Then use the oil to dress a black skull candle.
4. Write down your goals and desires on a piece of brown paper. It isn't necessary to write your name for this spell.
5. Light the candle. Scorch the paper in the flame and place it beneath an upturned saucer on which you then rest the candle.
6. When the candle has burned fairly low, light the paper in the flame and let it burn completely. Then, allow the candle to burn out.

EL NIÑO FIDENCIO

El Niño Fidencio, patron of illegals, ranks among Earth's great folk healers. He performed many miracles during his lifetime. Following his death in 1938, the miracles have continued. El Niño Fidencio's specialties are healing those with incurable illnesses and resolving immigration and deportation issues.

1. Burn copal incense in your bathroom, keeping doors and windows shut.
2. While the incense is burning, draw a warm bath. Add hibiscus flowers, yerba santa and essence of gardenia to the water.
3. When the incense has completed burning, allow the room to air out and then get into the bath.
4. Petition El Niño to intercede on your behalf, submerging yourself completely seven times. Promise El Niño Fidencio that you will repay his assistance by either visiting his shrine in Espinazo, Mexico or by helping someone else in similar circumstances when you are safe and able.

***

win a court case

You're in the right, but that's no guarantee. Add a little magic to tip the scales of justice in your favor.

LEGAL MOJO

Galangal root, also known as court case root, earned its nickname in the courthouse where it's reputed to ensure victory. Buy this cousin of ginger root in the supermarket under the name of Laos root, a staple of Indonesian cuisine. Yet another name for galangal is Chewing John. According to tradition, the root needs to be chewed and the juices spat out, typically in the direction of the judge and jury. Hoodoo doctors like the legendary Dr. Buzzard charged big bucks to sit front and center during a trial and chew. Spitting in public has become déclassé; a good mojo hand is equally effective and definitely more discreet!

1. Place a galangal root in a red-flannel drawstring bag

together with the herb deer's tongue (which bestows blessings of eloquence upon you and your attorney), calendula blossoms (to attract legal victories) and black poppy seeds (to confuse your enemies).
2. Carry the bag with you to court.

HOLD YOUR TONGUE!

Old and extremely popular, this spell is reputedly very effective. Variations abound but here's the basic ritual:
1. Write the names of the judge, lawyers, witnesses, your adversary, and anyone else who is your legal opponent on small, thin strips of paper about the size of the fortunes in fortune cookies.
2. With a sharp knife, cut slits into a beef tongue, insert the strips and sprinkle with vinegar and cayenne or habañero pepper powder.
3. Close the slits with pins.

At its simplest, the spell is now complete. Put the tongue in your freezer and leave it there for a year or until all danger is gone.

If a civil suit is threatened, don't freeze the tongue: Cook it instead. Boil it with garlic and salt. It's okay to leave out the pepper. Season it as you like it, because you'll be eating it.

Eat the paper, but don't eat the pins—remove them carefully. Do not throw them out in your home. Dispose of them far from your home, via a circuitous route. Return home via an equally circuitous route.

***

stay out of jail

Busted! Your immediate future doesn't look too bright. Call in some charmed reinforcements to stay out of the Big House.

FRIENDLY JUDGE OIL

1. Grind together one-half cup of carnation petals, one-quarter cup of anise seed and one-quarter cup of ground cinnamon.

2. Add one tablespoon of the powder to one ounce of sun-flower oil, reserving the rest for future use.
3. Add a piece of galangal root and a hematite crystal to the oil.
4. Add some of the oil to your bathwater on the three nights prior to your court appearance. Wear the oil to court. Prayer and petition might be in order, too!

HIGH JOHN'S TOBACCO SPELL

High John the Conqueror root is named after a legendary slave hero who always managed to stay one step ahead of disaster. Use his root charm to stay clear of the clutches of the law.

1. Finely chop a High John root and a galangal root.
2. Powder them with a mortar and pestle together with dried cloves, rosemary, and sage.
3. Add tobacco (buy it loose or unroll a cigarette) and a little salt to the mix. Blend well.

4. Reserve a little of the powder and then place the rest on a small charcoal as incense.
5. Carve your name, birthday, and the outcome you desire into the wax of a brown candle. Always write in the present tense. (For example: "I am acquitted.") Sprinkle the reserved powder on the top of the candle.
- Burn the candle and incense together while concentrating on your goals.
- Traditionally, this spell is accompanied by *intensive* repetitions of psalms.

***

protect your car

Your car has all the vulnerabilities of a home. Prevention is the key to safety: Use these spells before problems arise.

PRIZED METAL BOX

Papa Ogun, Spirit of Iron, emerged in Western Africa. He is considered to be the spiritual founder of civilization and progress. Although he didn't provide fire, Papa Ogun taught us what to do with it by creating the arts of forging metals and creating tools.

Ogun's powers are as double-edged as the proverbial sword. This spell appeases his appetites and invokes his blessings upon your personal box of metal, your car.

1. Obtain the finest cut of steak within your budget and go to your car.
2. Make your invocation:
   Papa Ogun, Father of Metal, helper of people
   Papa Ogun, swing your machete and cut a wide swathe of safety around this vehicle
   Please keep accidents, theft, break-ins and all danger far away from this car and it passengers
   Thank you Papa Ogun who provides sharp vision, sharp reflexes and protection
3. Rub the raw steak all over your car, concentrating on the

bumpers, tires or any other areas of concern.
4. If a dog unexpectedly appears and if it seems safe and appropriate, you may give the dog the steak. Otherwise dispose of it outside.
5. Wait a little while before washing your car.
- Ogun is traditionally most receptive on Wednesdays.
- Wearing the colors red, black, and/or green when approaching Ogun signifies your respect for him.
- Do not make offerings to Ogun when you are menstruating or bleeding in any way. In other words, if you fell or cut yourself shaving, leave the spell for another day.

MAXIMUM SAFETY AUTO AIR FRESHENER

Maybe you'd prefer a less primal approach? The fragrance of anise, used to attract helpful spirits, may also be used to promote auto safety.

1. Burn anise seeds as incense, wafting the smoke over your vehicle, both the interior and the exterior.
2. Repeat the process weekly as reinforcement.

***

avoid parking tickets

Now, of course we all know that the easiest way to avoid getting a ticket is to always obey parking laws and restrictions, right? But you have an emergency, you need your car, and the only parking you're likely to find is in the red zone. What can you do?

OGUN'S AUTO INCENSE

Did we mention that Ogun, patron of metal, also doubles as patron of police? This auto incense ideally induces cooperation among all involved parties. Worst-case scenario? Deer's tongue can help you talk your way out of the ticket!

1. Grind together Dragon's Blood resin, galangal root and the herb

deer's tongue using a mortar and pestle. When blended together, these herbs allegedly keep law enforcement officers at a distance.
2. Dragon's Blood is strongly associated with Ogun. Feel free to incorporate a petition to him for protection while grinding. For maximum emphasis, use a metal mortar and pestle.
3. Sprinkle the herbs on a charcoal or light them in a cast-iron pan in your car and fumigate your vehicle thoroughly.
4. Take a little of each botanical, place it in a red-flannel drawstring bag and hide the bag in your car as a safety talisman.

AUTO FENG SHUI: OPEN THE SPACE

The techniques of feng shui, most commonly used to protect the home and office, can also be applied to protecting your car and improving your driving. The ba gua is an octagonal image frequently used as a feng shui remedy and safety device. When attached to your car, it's reputed to open up the flow of traffic, including freeing parking spaces! Feng shui supply outlets sell adhesive ba gua stickers. Place one on the rear bumper. It also reputedly wards off road rage and other unpleasant motoring experiences.

***

protect your computer

Stop trouble before it occurs: Prevention is the best medicine. Use magical means to ward off glitches, hackers, viruses and crashes.

A SORCERER'S COMPUTER SCREEN

Erect a protective screen around your computer with images and devices specifically attuned to the technology. Try some or all of these magical protection techniques:
1. Put a bell on or near the computer and ring it at least once during use.

2. Prominently display the color cobalt.
3. Snakes are the computer's animal allies. Images and representations of snakes and dragons placed on or near your computer keep the treasures stored within your computer safe from prying eyes.

> There are snakes and there are *snakes!* The Congolese water spirit, Simbi, most commonly manifests as a great snake. Simbi rules crossroads, transmissions, conductivity, and communications. This ancient spirit has found a new calling as a guardian of communications technology, including computers. Simbi gets thirsty: Feed him water and whisky daily (in separate dishes) and request his assistance in keeping your communications smooth and flowing.

MERCURY OIL

The ancient Greek spirit Hermes, in the guise of his Roman counterpart

Mercury, is patron of modern communication technologies like telephones, televisions, and especially computers. Request his assistance to keep problems at a minimum.
1. Concoct *Mercury Oil* by blending the essential oils of lavender, peppermint, and thyme.
2. Add the oil to a spray bottle filled with spring water.
3. Spray around the computer area twice daily (never directly on the computer!). You may also lightly spray the oil on a cloth and carefully wipe down your computer and the surrounding area. Just be careful not to damage the computer!

***

protect your pet

A beloved animal companion is like a child or a best friend. He or she deserves all the protection you can muster.

ANIMAL GUARDIAN ANGELS

Animals have spirit guardians, too. Don't hesitate to call in these powerful protectors whenever they're needed:
- Hecate: dogs and frogs
- Atargatis: fish
- Anat: horses
- Bastet: cats
- Lilith: snakes
- Aphrodite: all creatures

1. Light a white candle that you've dressed with frankincense. Speak respectfully, addressing the appropriate spirit, offering words similar to the following:
   I am the caretaker for one of your children,
   I appeal to you for aid and assistance,
   Protect (pet's name)
   Please guide me to make the right decisions and take the correct actions on her/his behalf

Tell the spirit immediately that you have petitioned because you know that it's best to take every opportunity to safeguard the animal you both love. (Be respectful: Lilith and Anat, in particular, can be quite temperamental.)

2. Using your candle's flame, light a lavender smudge wand and use its smoke to demarcate an area of protected space around your pet.

THE GREEN CAT OF GOOD HEALTH

A candle that accurately depicts your pet is ideal, of course, and candle stores sometimes do sell very specifically detailed candles. If you can't find such a candle, green cat-shaped candles have traditionally been used to petition for any animal's good health and safety.

1. Carve your pet's name and other identifying information into the wax.
2. Add essences of lavender, lemon, patchouli, and vetiver to jojoba oil and dress the candle with the oil.
3. Start burning the candle when trouble of any kind first appears.

The candle must be burned for thirty minutes at a time and then the flames should be extinguished. You may burn the candle multiple times during the day or you may burn the candle once daily.
4. If the candle burns out and the problem still hasn't been resolved, it's time to reassess measures taken and explore other alternatives.
5. Should the crisis be completely resolved before the candle is completely burned, dispose of the remainder of the candle outside your home. Do not use it again. In the event of a new emergency, start with a fresh candle.

***

fly the friendly skies

While some people find any kind of travel stressful, air travel tends to evoke the most intense feelings of vulnerability. Use these charms to ensure safety and the sunniest skies possible!

SWALLOW'S BLOOD SAFETY POWDER

Don't worry! There are no spells in this book that involve harming little birds! This powder is named for its color and to honor swallows, birds flamed for the length of their annual migrations.
1. Grind together Dragon's Blood resin, red sandalwood powder, red rose petals, and orris root.
2. Sprinkle the powder on charcoal and fumigate yourself, your traveling clothes, and your luggage for safety and security.

TRAVELER'S TALISMAN

Swallow's blood powder made you feel better *before* you got on the plane. But now here you are sitting tensely in your seat, worrying about crashing, worrying about your fellow passengers, wishing that there was *something* at hand that would bring a sense of ease.

- Mugwort has been a traveler's talisman for thousands of years, long before the advent of airplanes. It's extended its power to provide protection during modern modes of transportation.
- A mere twig of mugwort grants safety and spiritual assistance. For safe passage, tuck a little into your bra or pocket.

***

smooth sailing

Traveling over water? This ancient form of travel can incite ancient, primal anxieties. Feeling alone, nervous, and vulnerable in the midst of open waters? Earth's vast expanses of water shelter an abundance of powerful spirits: keep on their good side!

POSEIDON'S GOOD LUCK CHARM

This talisman is based on ancient Coptic magic and invokes the protection of the ancient Lord of the Mediterranean.

1. Draw a picture of Poseidon, ruler of the sea, earthquakes, and tidal waves. He is a handsome man of indeterminate age with a flowing beard. He brandishes a trident. Your image must depict him rising from the sea with one foot on a dolphin. Artistic ability isn't important. What *is* vital is that while you're drawing, you single-mindedly focus on the safety and smooth sailing the talisman is intended to bring.
2. Activate the talisman at the time of the New Moon by anointing the corners of the paper with essential oil of pine, Poseidon's sacred tree.
3. Invoke his protection:
Lord Poseidon, bring to me,
Sunny skies, gentle waves,
Fun, safety and security!

4. Hide your talisman somewhere on the boat.

SAFE PASSAGE

The Lord and Lady of the Western Waters, Agwé and his wife, the mermaid La Sirène, are traditionally petitioned to protect boats. Create a shrine aboard the vessel you want them to protect.

1. Place offerings of sea glass and seashells for Agwé into a miniature boat. You can use a toy boat or construct one. It can be elaborate or simple, depending upon your artistic capacity. If necessary, construct a boat from popsicle sticks.
2. Place offerings of pearls, a mirror, and a comb for La Sirène alongside the little boat.
3. Offer a shallow dish filled with plain, still, spring water for freshwater journeys or salted water for ocean journeys.
4. Give Agwé and La Sirène each a glass of champagne.
5. Pour a glass for yourself: Toast the sacred pair and your journey. Tell them where you're going, why you're going and assure them that you mean their

waters and their creatures no harm. (If this is not the case, you may want to reconsider this spell—or better yet, your journey.) Ask them very nicely for their assistance and protection.

***

keep your hair on

Do you remember the story of Samson and Delilah? Delilah betrayed Samson to his enemies when she revealed that his awesome strength would be broken if his never-shorn hair was cut. Hair does more than just protect your scalp from the sun and attract romantic attention. Traditional occult wisdom considers hair an advertisement of your personal power. Keep it abundant, in the right places.

HAIR GROWTH STIMULATION FORMULA

Here's an aromatic approach to growing it:

1. Blend twelve drops each of the essential oils of rosemary and ylang ylang.
2. Blend one-half ounce of castor oil with one-half ounce of jojoba oil and add the essential oils.
3. Massage your scalp with the growth stimulation formula every night before retiring.

ONION HEAD

Onions have a strong association with virility and masculine good health. When ingested, they're said to protect the heart. When rubbed on the head, they allegedly stimulate hair growth.

If enough of your scalp is exposed, you can use the traditional Anglo-Saxon method:
1. Cut an onion in half.
2. Vigorously rub the inside of the onion (the cut side) over your scalp twice daily, in the morning and evening.

If you have too much hair to rub the onion over your scalp:

1. Juice an onion and blend it with a shot of vodka and a tablespoon of honey.
2. Massage the mixture into your scalp; leave it on for thirty minutes, then shampoo.

***

stay healthy during an epidemic

This classic formula has traditionally been used to fortify the immune system and ward off infectious illness.

Some say it happened in England, others in France, or Italy.

Some say the incident occurred during the thirteenth century, others that it was more recent. This much, however, is generally acknowledged to be true:

Europe was wracked with devastating contagious plagues. Fear ran rampant. Panic ruled the streets. Quarantines were brutally enforced.

In the midst of this chaos, four thieves stole with impunity, robbing bodies, ransacking quarantined homes.

How could they stoop so low, people wondered. More importantly, how did they avoid getting sick themselves?

Inevitably, the thieves were caught. The crowds clamored for their blood. Sentenced to death, they cut a deal: Their lifesaving formula for one-way tickets out of town. Their secret was revealed: Four Thieves Vinegar.

FOUR THIEVES VINEGAR

The recipe for this vinegar has almost as many variations as its legend. Like the legend, though, there is a consistent basis to the recipe:

Peel and bruise garlic cloves and add them to one quart of apple cider or red wine vinegar. How much garlic? As much as you want. It's virtually impossible to have too much.

The variables: Whole cayenne pepper,[5] lavender, mint, rosemary, rue, sage, thyme, and wormwood.

---

[5] Cayenne peppers resemble horns, emphasizing their protective capacity. For a spicier favor, make slits in the pepper before adding to the vinegar base; for a milder favor, keep the pepper intact.

1. Choose one ingredient from the above list of variables to represent each thief's contribution to the potion. There should be four in all.
2. Add them to the vinegar and shake it vigorously.
3. Allow the potion to steep in a cool, dark place for seven days.
4. A tablespoon or two a day is said to keep the doctor away, although some recommend as much as a glass daily. It can also be used as a salad dressing.

> *Four Thieves Vinegar* also has magical uses, mostly for protection and banishment and is a component of many spells. See Marie Laveau's banishing spell.

***

get well soon!

Is it too late for prevention? If you or someone dear to you is very ill, these spells can be used to reinforce any medical treatment.

FOR THE BIRDS

"Babalu Ayé" means "Father of the Earth." It's the term of respect used to address a spirit so great and terrible many of his devotees fear to utter his true name. Lord of suffering, smallpox and other epidemics, Babalu both delivers and relieves contagious illnesses. Request his sympathy and assistance if you need a cure.

1. Create a simple shrine for Babalu by laying down a raffia cloth.
2. Call him with an offering of good white wine (never offer him water) plus a bowl of milk in which you have placed a slice of bread to feed his constant companions, his beloved dogs who exemplify eternal loyalty. Place the wine and the milk onto the raffia.
3. Pour palm oil over a bowl of popcorn. Place this on the cloth, too. The glass of wine and the bowl of milk with bread may be

removed within twenty-four hours but the bowl of oil-covered popcorn *must* stand on the cloth for seventeen days.
4. Use your shrine as a focal point for petition and prayer.
5. When the seventeen days have passed, take the popcorn to a park and feed it to the birds. Do not leave your shrine standing unless it is actively in use. No need to draw Babalu's attention for any longer than necessary.

SLEEP AWAY THAT SICKNESS!

Children's illnesses are a uniquely painful source of heartache. This Arabic spell is cast to help a child heal.
1. Place seven fat breads (pita or lavash style) beneath the pillow of a very ill child.
2. Leave them there as the child sleeps, either overnight or for an equivalent period of time.
3. When the child awakens, remove the bread from your house and feed it to birds or stray dogs.

***

survive natural disasters

There are two approaches for dealing with natural disasters: Prevention and protection.

PREVENTION

First, consider what kinds of disasters have a genuine possibility of occurring. Take steps to protect yourself by implementing conventional safety recommendations. Next, turn to *Fiery Wall of Protection Oil* for reinforcement and spiritual protection. Sprinkle the formula throughout your home once a month, at the time of the new moon. Concentrate on doorways, windows, thresholds, closets and corners, plus all of the places you think are vulnerable, whether that's based on intuition or fact.

For triple-strength protection, add *Fiery Wall of Protection Oil* to a bucket of water and vinegar. Wash down your walls and scrub your floors and front steps with the mixture.

CALLING ALL ANGELS!

When it's too late for prevention, it's time to call in the experts!

Each archangel is affiliated with a particular direction. These directions are used to summon the archangels with greater clarity, although rest assured, their protection emerges from all corners!

1. Stand in the center of the room, in the spot that symbolizes the heart of your dwelling.
2. Turn to the north and call for Uriel, angel of wisdom and insight. (Call him like you mean it. Call his name aloud!)
3. Then, turn to the east and call in Raphael, the angel of healing.
4. Turn to the south to call Michael, the warrior angel.
5. Finally, turn to the west and call in Gabriel, the performer of miracles.
6. When you feel yourself surrounded by the archangels (as each archangel commands a host, they may show up alone or with a crowd), speak from

your heart and say what you need.

***

soothe savage beasts

You're in the woods and you're terrified you'll encounter a wild beast up close and personal. First question: Why are you even in their territory? The areas where animals may freely roam have become so circumscribed, can you really blame territorial behavior? Be that as it may, here you are, in need of safe passage.

ARTEMIS' PASSPORT TO THE WILD

Once upon a time, good manners required that you request permission to enter the wilderness.

Artemis is the divine sponsor of humans who hunt and the caretaker of all wild creatures. She is the arbiter of disputes, the maintainer of sacred balance. When you request her protection, tell her that you love and respect the wild as she does and wish it no harm but wish no harm to befall you, either. Create a talisman to serve as her passport to protection.

Use twigs, dried roots or any part of the plants mugwort, wormwood, and sweet Annie, all herbs belonging to the botanical genus *Artemisia,* named in her honor. Charge them with your desire under the full moon and then place them in a white or unbleached cotton drawstring bag along with a small bit of real silver. Carry it with you during your adventures!

KLUDDE OIL

Kludde is a shape-shifting Belgian goblin, a fairly foul-tempered Rumpelstiltskin type. One of the more unpleasant spirits, he is reputedly able to assume the form of any creature he chooses, including cute little kitty cats, the better to lure people to their death in the woods. The condition oil that bears his name, however, is alleged to keep one safe from all creatures, including other humans.

1. Concoct some *Kludde Oil* by mixing the essential oils of citronella grass, fir, and pine with castor oil.
2. Anoint the palms of your hands and the soles of your shoes with the oil. You may also use it to anoint any other lucky charms you carry for added reinforcement.

> True worst-case scenario? Agate allegedly speeds the healing of scorpion and snake bites, as well as injuries inflicted by other animals. Carry one in your pocket to enhance the healing process.

***

lose a stalker

Is someone following you? This is among the creepiest and most urgent emergencies of all.

BOLDO BANISHING SOLUTION

Boldo is an evergreen tree native to South America. Its leaves are reputed to repel stalkers.

1. Grind up boldo leaves and combine them with asafetida, sulfur powder and powdered chilé peppers.
2. Add this to arrowroot powder and mix well.
3. Sprinkle this mixture in the path of the person whom you want to stop pursuing you. Also sprinkle it on any ports of entry into your residence or place of work (windows, doors, or any place that you sense may be vulnerable).

VAN VAN VANISHING ACT

1. Add graveyard dirt to protective *Van Van Oil,* preferably from the grave of someone who loves you and would protect you with her or his life. If collecting actual graveyard dirt isn't feasible,

ground patchouli and/or valerian leaves mixed with any old plain dirt can substitute for the real thing.
2. Add the oil to a wide-nozzle spray bottle filled with spring water. Spray the oil on yourself. Or, alternatively, paint it on yourself using a pastry brush.
3. Also use the oil to anoint an angelica root, which should be carried between your breasts.

> Life can be complicated: Although you want to avoid a particular person, you may also wish to attract others. If the stalking situation is serious, be wise: Do not carry lodestones or wear any sort of attraction oil until the situation is completely resolved.

***

turn an enemy into an ally

Wouldn't it be easier if we all got along? This is particularly true when your success depends upon an enemy's cooperation.

NOW LOVE ME BATH

Although all botanicals possess some kind of power, some are exceptionally potent. At the top of the list is vervain. Vervain bears many gifts. One is the ability to transform an enemy into a friend.

1. Make an infusion from dried vervain and orris root.
2. Add it to a tub of warm water. Just before entering the bath, add essential oils of myrrh and sandalwood.
3. Bathe, completely immersing yourself in the water.
4. With a clean towel, pat yourself dry as minimally as is safe and comfortable. Leave yourself just a little damp.
5. The fragrance of the oil that lingers on your skin should inspire the affection of those with whom you come into contact. Repeat the ritual daily or as needed.

EASE YOUR WRATH POWDER

It can get very scary when someone intensely hates or dislikes you. This formula allegedly eliminates feelings of animosity toward you.

1. Compose a letter, on joss or brown paper, detailing *why* the enmity should turn to friendship. Explain how, given the opportunity, you could be good friends. (OK, maybe polite acquaintances.)
2. Burn the paper completely, down to smoke and ashes.
3. Reserve the ashes and mix them up with rose petals, sandalwood powder and sweet Hungarian paprika. Add six drops of essential oil of jasmine and allow the powder to dry.
4. Toss the powder onto your enemy. Does the notion of tossing something onto your enemy strike you as foolhardy and dangerous? It is the traditional and recommended

approach, but here are some more cautious alternatives in their order of preference:
- Add a handful of cornstarch to the ash powder and blend it all thoroughly. Put it in a plastic bag, take it to your enemy's home or workplace and sprinkle the powder on the ground where he or she is bound to step over it.
- Place the ash powder in the palm of your hand. Visualize your hope of peace and friendship, then blow a little powder in all directions.

> You might also try giving your enemy a present. Chocolate reputedly holds the power to soften hearts; offering a gift of a good box may turn the trick!

***

banish bad dreams

Do daytime troubles pale in comparison to the terrors that stalk you at night? Sleep is necessary to survival. When you're afraid to close your eyes, everything in your life suffers.

HOUSEHOLD HELP

Even when nightmares afflict only one person, they can keep the whole household awake. As long as everyone's up, you may as well have a nightmare-banishing party! This spell requires group effort.

1. Slowly melt wax in a double boiler.
2. With the nightmare victim seated, everyone present should pray and petition aloud for the nightmares to be understood and dispelled.
3. Have one person hold a clean white cloth (a tea towel, for example) over the nightmare sufferer's head.
4. Have someone else hold a dish of ice-cold water over the cloth.

5. Have another person pour the molten wax into the water. It should begin to harden immediately.
6. When it cools, remove the wax pieces and allow the dreamer to analyze their shapes. Afterward, others may contribute their own interpretations but it is important that the person plagued by the nightmares goes first.
7. Wrap the wax fragments in the tea towel and dispose of both far from home.

NIGHTMARES, BE GONE!

The herbs in this dream pillow allegedly prevent and banish nightmares.
1. Place one piece of muslin atop another of identical size.
2. Stitch together three sides of the cloth leaving one end open.
3. Turn the little bag inside out so that the seams are inside the pillow.

4. Fill the pillow with a combination of anise seeds, dried calendula blossoms and dried mullein.
5. Sew the pillow shut. If you like, you may also make a pillow cover to go on top of the dream pillow. (That pillow cover can be washed; the dream pillow itself can't be washed without first removing the herbs.)
6. Keep the pillow close enough to you that you can smell its fragrance while you sleep.

> For extra fortification, wearing a piece of jade at night is said to cure bad dreams. Coral has an affinity for children; many cultures use it to ease children's night terrors.

***

invoke the dead

If only you had thought to ask Aunt Rita where she kept the key to her safe-deposit box. It's too late now that she's dead. Or is it?

LADY CIRCE: TOUR GUIDE TO THE OTHER WORLD

You can converse with people who have passed during waking visions but this involves difficult and stressful techniques. You may need a capable spiritual tour guide to the world beyond. Request assistance from that supreme shaman, Lady Circe.

1. Sprinkle ground cinnamon on a dish of honey and stir.
2. Stick a peeled garlic clove into the honey and surround the dish with toy animals.
3. Invoke Circe for her help (she appreciates flattery).
4. Place dried mugwort and dittany of Crete in a cast-iron pot and set them alight. Experiment with quantities: A substantial amount of botanicals may be required to maintain a good flame and plenty of smoke.
5. With a feather, a fan, or your hands, waft the smoke over you and inhale the fragrance.

6. Stare into the center of the flame, keep your mind blank and await visitation. Don't be discouraged if you don't succeed the first time. Repeat until success is achieved.

CONTACT THE DEAD DREAM INCENSE

The simpler way to communicate with the dearly departed is within dreams. Of course, you need to prime yourself for contact first.

1. Grind together star anise, acacia leaves, frankincense, myrrh, and sandalwood powder.
2. Close your bedroom's windows and doors. Sprinkle the powder on charcoal and burn it as incense, concentrating the fragrance near the bed.
3. Once the incense has burned out, aerate the room and go to sleep.
4. If you cannot sleep, just lie quietly, keeping your mind as free of thought as possible and

focusing on the lingering fragrance.
- It's best to get into the habit of remembering and recording your dreams.
- Repeat as necessary.

***

locate missing persons

This is the classic scenario that causes even doubters to turn to a psychic for help. Awaken your own psychic skills and locate your missing person.

A COMPASS CANDLE

A compass candle can point your search in the right direction. It's unlikely, however, that you'll find anything marketed under that name. What you're looking for are especially drippy tapers, the type traditionally placed in wicker-wrapped Chianti bottles which, when burned, form rivers of wax.
1. Hold the unlit candle in both hands. Silently charge the candle with its search mission.

2. Place the candle in a holder resting on a flat surface. Establish the directions of north, south, east, and west. They don't have to coincide with the real compass points: All that's important is that you and any other observers know which side of the candle represents north. Make sure you all agree so as to avoid arguments or doubt.
3. The candle will tell you where to begin searching by spilling the most wax on that side. In-between drippings signify in-between directions; for instance, if most of the wax spills between the points designated north and east, initiate your search to the northeast. The missing person may or may not be *found* in that direction. The candle only advises you of the direction in which it is most beneficial to direct your search. Start there and follow any trail you find.

A clear answer will be obvious. If a clear direction cannot be determined, this too is an answer: The situation is a mess, the direction is unclear, some piece of information is missing.

SANDALWOOD SEARCH

Sandalwood's aroma is a component of sacred rituals worldwide. Its fragrance is reputed to stimulate visions of beloved ones far away.

1. Burn sandalwood powder as incense, deeply inhaling the fumes. Try to concentrate on the aroma and allow thoughts to jump unbidden into your head.
2. Alternately, fill a bowl with boiling water. Add twelve drops of essential oil of sandalwood. Drape a towel over your head like a tent and lean over the steaming bowl.
3. Don't actively think about finding the person; instead, just focus on the aroma. Let thoughts just jump into your mind.

For best results, do this before going to sleep. Make an effort to sleep but do not use artificial sleep aids, which stifle dreams. Dreaming is the psychic route of greatest ease. If you can't sleep, lie still, keep your mind clear, focus on your breathing and simply allow information to approach you, if and when it will.

***

rescue distant loved ones

Someone you love is in trouble. Your assistance is desperately needed but you're too far away to help. Or are you?

MENTAL TELEPHONE

If you badly want to help but don't know what to do, let the person tell you. Establish a line of mental communication so they can send you messages, request assistance, and tell you what they need you to do. This isn't an easy technique, so it's best to practice telepathy with your loved ones just for fun so you'll be ready just in case an emergency ever arises.

1. For practice: Take turns sending and receiving messages. The sender concentrates on

transmitting a clear, simple message to the other person. (As your skills improve, the messages can become increasingly complex, if you like, but start simple.) The receiver stays still and just allows thoughts and visions to pop into their head. Compare notes and see if you've achieved a psychic connection.

2. Some people can establish a mental connection without the help of magical tools but many find using a crystal ball or pan of water as a scrying device to be very helpful. The tools potentially benefit the person receiving the messages.

3. If you're using a crystal or pan of water, gaze into it with your eyes slightly unfocused. Keep your mind clear and let thoughts arise unbidden.

> It's vital to distinguish between panic and inspiration. This can be a difficult spell but when it works, it's invaluable!

ANGEL ALERT!

When you can't get there to help, send the most powerful reinforcements possible to serve in your stead.

1. Get the largest white candle you can find.
2. Carve your name and birthday, as well as those belonging to whomever needs your help, into the candle.
3. Add five drops each of the essential oils of spikenard, myrrh, sandalwood, and frankincense to a quarter-cup of olive oil. Dress your candle with the oil.
4. Place the candle in a dish filled with sea salt.
5. Write your heart's desire on a piece of paper. Place it under the candle and light the wick.
6. Summon the archangels. Call them by name, turning to face the appropriate directions:

Look north to call Uriel, the angel of wisdom; east to summon Raphael, the angel of healing; south for Michael,

the angel of defense and west to call Gabriel, the angel of miracles.
7. Speak to them from your heart. Remind them that your loved one needs assistance and vigilance from all corners and all directions.

***

you're lost! find your way

You're lost, you don't know which way to turn. If you're alone, you may be feeling especially vulnerable. If you're with another, you're probably at each other's throats. Use magical means to set your compass. These spells may be used to provide either physical or spiritual direction.

IT MUST BE THIS WAY!

Based on gbo amulets from the Dahomey region of Africa, this charm is reputed to keep its bearer moving in the right direction.
1. Roll and stitch together a red-flannel cloth, leaving it hollow inside, into a shape that

approximates that of a pointing finger.
2. Stuff it with earth, coal powder, and a small piece of real silver.
3. Sew it closed and carry it on your person.

> If you find yourself traveling alone at night, repeating Psalm 121 seven times is reputed to help you safely reach your destination.

NO TRICKS, I'M TRAVELING!

Hermes, an ancient Greek divinity, rules tricks, travels, and communication. Ask for his help when you don't know which way to turn.
1. Pull over in a safe spot and stop the car if you're driving. If you're on foot, find a discreet place of refuge for a moment.
2. Shut your eyes tightly. Plug your ears with your fingers to drown out all sound. Quickly petition Hermes: Tell him you're lost, you're scared, and you need him

to point you in the right direction.
3. When you're done, open your eyes and unplug your ears. The first sounds or words you hear are your celestial directions. If you're in the car, turn on the radio.

***

find missing objects

Lost your keys? Lost your car? These spells will you track them down.

A QUICK FIX

1. Put your left hand against the side of your head by your ear with your thumb pressed against your head and your palm facing forward.
2. Clear your mind of worry and thoughts. Visualize your hand projecting a magnetic force that draws objects toward you. This gesture evokes Maneki Neko, the Japanese beckoning cat of good fortune. No, it's unlikely that

your hand will literally be magnetized. (Never say never, but let's face facts!) The gesture does exert a draw, however. Don't be surprised if your missing object turns up close at hand fairly quickly!

SAN CIPRIANO OIL

San Cipriano, Bishop of Carthage, had an interesting career. An early pillar of the Roman Catholic Church, he was also a flamed wizard and exorcist. His mystic reputation remains vibrant; he is the patron saint of magicians. The condition oil named in his honor is reputed to stimulate the return of lost objects.

Dress a brown candle with *San Cipriano Oil* (cinnamon powder, Low John powder,[6] orris root, essential oils

---

[6] Many plant species, including Low John, also known as bethroot (Trillium erectum) are endangered. Although it is a component of the original formula, if you can't find it or have doubts about whether it was gathered ethically, just leave it out. The formula is powerful enough without

of cedar and cypress, and either myrrh resin or essential oil of myrrh in a castor oil base) and then light it.

1. Concentrate on a vision of yourself reunited with what you have lost.
2. On a square of brown paper, distinctly describe and/or name the item that needs to be found.
3. Singe the paper in the candle's flame and call the object aloud.
4. Do this for fifteen minutes, then extinguish the candle's flame by pinching or snuffing (*not* blowing it out.)
5. Repeat for fifteen minutes daily until the object is located or the candle burns out.
6. If the candle burns out before the object is found, the message is for you to reassess how, why, and where you think it was lost.

***

it and unethical gathering of plants may create a backfire effect. For optimum power and security, cultivate your own supply of the plant and any others.

help someone help you

Feeling desperate and alone? Maybe you can't get in touch with the person whose help you need the most? You know she or he would help, if only you could communicate what needs to be done. Use these techniques to conjure up assistance.

THE MIND'S LIFELINE

This spell requires only your focused mind. No oils, no candles, no other stuff. An exercise in concentration, this may be the hardest spell in this book. If it doesn't work right away, don't get discouraged: Practice and *concentrate!*

1. Conjure up the image of the person whose help you need.
2. The image must be three-dimensional and show the entire person from head to toe. You must be able to visualize the person as clearly as if he or she were standing in front of you.
3. When you've conjured the image, hold it firm and talk to it. Be

brief and to the point; deliver all pertinent information concisely. Then, slowly allow the image to fade.

LETTER OF ASSISTANCE

1. Write a letter to the person whose help you need. Keep the letter short and to the point but include as many details as are necessary. Tell the person what he or she needs to know to help you.
2. Place the letter in an envelope and address it to the person. Don't worry about whether you have the complete address or whether it's entirely accurate. This is a spirit letter, there's no need to worry about postal requirements.
3. Carve your name, birthday, and present location into a candle.
4. Dress it with essential oil of sandalwood and light the candle. Singe the letter in the flame and then place it below the candle.

When the candle burns out, do not dispose of the wax. Instead, wrap any remaining wax and paper into a cloth and keep it hidden near you. Make sure the letter is illegible to human eyes, however. If the wax and flames haven't already rendered it unreadable, rip it into tiny bits or burn it down to ashes, all the while concentrating on your goal.

***

bonus spell: obtain your heart's desire

Perhaps your emergency is unique and fits no category. Maybe a spell has yet to be devised. Then again, maybe it's not simply a matter of an emergency. Sometimes we possess a secret desire, something or someone we crave so urgently, with a yearning that cannot be articulated or expressed aloud.

ANGELS OF THE AIR, FULFILL MY WISH

1. Blend the essential oils of cinnamon, frankincense, patchouli and vetiver and add them to a tablespoon of jojoba oil. (Only one or two drops of each essential oil is necessary.)
2. Use the oil to dress a red candle.
3. Place a horseshoe[7] around the candle with the open end toward you.
4. Write your wish on a piece of paper, stating it as clearly, concisely, and precisely as you can.
5. Fold the paper over twice, forming a square shape.
6. Make your wish—either silently or aloud—and light the candle.

---

[7] For utmost power, a horseshoe is magically activated only by being attached to a horse's hoof. Many stables and ranches will be happy to give you a used one or sell you one for a minimal charge.

7. Using tweezers, put the paper to the flame. (Don't burn your fingers!)
8. Visualize yourself happy, your wish come true.
9. Burn the paper until every last letter is gone.
10. The spell is now complete, but for extra impact remain with the candle until it burns out, all the while visualizing the fulfillment of your desire.

a psychic shopper's guide

Support your local merchants! If you can find quality products, patronize your neighbors. If that isn't possible, however, the following have proved extremely reputable and helpful. Asterisks indicate that ready-made condition oils, made from authentic materials, are available.

Aphrodisia

264 Bleecker Street
New York, NY 10012
212-989-6440
www.aphrodisiaherbshoppe.com
Extensive selection of botanicals and oils

Enfeurage

321 Bleecker Street
New York, NY 10014
212-691-1610
www.enfeurage.com
Extensive selection of essential oils

Island of Salvation Botanica*

835 Piety Street
New Orleans, LA 70117
504-948-9961
www.feyvodou.com
sallieann@earthlink.net
Botanicals, charms, candles, and spells

Kyphi Aromatherapy, Inc.

327 Renfrew Drive, Suite 102
Markham, ON
Canada L3R 958
416-383-1586
www.kyphiinc.com
email: info@kyphiinc.com
Essential oils, true oils and dried herbs, many from Egypt

John Steele/Lifetree Aromatix

3949 Longridge Avenue
Sherman Oaks, CA 91423
818-986-0594

Extensive selection of essential oils

Mountain Rose Herbs

P.O. Box 50220
Eugene, OR 97405
www.mountainroseherbs.com
Within the US: 800-879-3337
Outside the US: 541-741-7307
Extensive selection of botanicals,
 essential and true oils

Scully Elly's Voodoo Joint*

P.O. Box 770380
New Orleans, LA 70177-0380
504-944-7536
www.thejukejoint.com
Botanicals, charms, spells, and great
 music, too!

For Statues of Deities

The Guiding Tree

4831 SE Division Street
Portland, OR 97206

503-239-7458
www.theguidingtree.com

Sacred Source

P.O. Box 163WW
Crozet, VA 22932
800-290-6203
www.sacredsource.com

For Flower Essence Remedies

Australian Bush Flower Essences

45 Booralie Road
Terrey Hills, NSW
2084, Australia
www.ausflowers.com.au
email: info@ausflowers.com.au

The Dr. Edward Bach Centre

Mount Vernon, Bakers Lane
Brightwell-cum-Sotwell, Oxon, OX10 0P2

United Kingdom
www.bachcentre.com

Flower Essence Services (FES)

P.O. Box 1769
Nevada City, CA 95959
800-548-0075
www.fesflowers.com (products)
www.flowersociety.org (education and research)

Green Hope Farm, LLC

P.O. Box 125
Meriden, NH 03770
603-469-3662
www.greenhopeessences.com

Pegasus Products

P.O. Box 228
Boulder, CO 80306
303-652-3424
www.pegasusproducts.com

Books for Further Information

Pure Magic: A Complete Course in Spellcasting
Judika Illes
Weiser Books, San Francisco, California 2007

The Aromatherapy Book
Jeanne Rose
North Atlantic Books, Berkeley, California, 1992

The Flower Remedy Book: A Comprehensive Guide to Over 700 Flower Essences
Jeffery Garson Shapiro
North Atlantic Books, Berkeley, California, 1999

botanical classifications

Plants may have many common names or nicknames. Some nicknames, like graveyard dust, apply to more than one plant. However, a Latin scientific name applies exclusively to only one plant species; rely on the Latin name for safety, security and enhanced magic power.

acacia *Acacia spp.*
allspice *Pimento officinalis*
amyris *Amyris balsamifera*
angelica *Angelica archangelica*
anise *Pimpinella anisum*
asafetida *Ferula assa-foetida*
balm of Gilead *Populus candicans*
bay laurel *Laurus nobilis*
benzoin *Styrax benzoin*
bergamot *Citrus aurantium spp. Bergamia*
black pepper *Piper nigrum*
boldo *Peumus boldus*
borage *Borago officinalis*
calendula *Calendula officinalis*
camphor *Cinnamomum camphora*
cardamom *Elettaria cardomomum*
carnation *Dianthus caryophyllus*

catnip *Nepeta cataria*
cayenne pepper *Capsicum frutescens*
chamomile, German *Matricaria chamomilla*
chamomile, Roman *Anthemis nobilis*
cinnamon *Cinnamomum zeylanicum*
citronella *Cymbopogon nardus*
clary sage *Salvia sclarea*
clove *Eugenia caryophyllus*
coriander *Coriandrum sativum*
cumin *Cuminum cyminum*
cypress *Cupressus sempervirens*
damiana *Turnera aphrodisiaca*
deer's tongue *Liatris odoratissima*
devil's shoestring *Viburnum spp.*
dittany of Crete *Origanum dictamnus*
Dragon's Blood *Daemonorops draco*
fennel *Foeniculum vulgare*
fenugreek *Trigonella foenum-graecum*
fir *Abies spp.*
five-finger grass *Potentilla reptans*
frankincense *Boswellia carterii*
galangal *Alpinia galanga*
gardenia *Gardenia spp.*

gingergrass *Cymbopogon martinii var. sofia*
grapefruit *Citrus paradisi*
gravel root *Eupatorium purpureum*
hibiscus *Hibiscus spp.*
High John the Conqueror *Ipomoea jalapa*
hops *Humulus lupulus*
hydrangea *Hydrangea arborescens*
hyssop *Hyssopus officinalis*
immortelle *Helichrysum spp.*
lavender *Lavandula officinalis*
lemongrass *Cymbopogon citratus*
licorice root *Glycyrrhiza glabra*
mother of thyme *Thyme serpyllum*
mugwort *Artemisia vulgaris*
mullein *Verbascum thapsus*
myrrh *Commiphora myrrha*
neroli *Citrus aurantium var. bigarade*
orange *Citrus sinensis*
oregano *Origanum vulgare*
orris root *Iris germanica*
palmarosa *Cymbopogon martinii var. stapf*
patchouli *Pogostemon cablin*
peppermint *Mentha piperita*
petitgrain *Citrus aurantium var. amara*

pine *Pinus spp.*
poke root *Phytolacca decandra*
rose *Rosa spp.*
rosemary *Rosmarinus officinalis*
St. John's wort *Hypericum perforatum*
sandalwood *Santalum album*
sandalwood, red *Adenanthera pavonina*
sassafras *Sassafras officinale*
slippery elm *Ulmus fulva*
spearmint *Mentha spicata*
spikenard *Nardostachys jatamansi*
star anise *Illicium verum*
sweet Annie *Artemisia annua*
sweet flag (calamus) *Acorus calamus*
thyme *Thymus vulgaris*
tonka bean *Dipteryx odorata*
valerian *Valeriana officinalis*
vervain *Verbena officinalis*
vetiver *Vetiveria zizanoides*
wormwood *Artemisia absinthium*
yerba santa *Eriodictyon spp.*
ylang ylang *Cananga odorata*

acknowledgments

First and foremost, thanks to Greg Brandenburgh, present at the conception and at the resurrection. I offer my gratitude and appreciation to Jan Johnson of Red Wheel/Weiser Books. Marianne Carroll, Theresa Mannino, Carole Murray, Holly Schmidt, Wendy Simard, Jeff Theis, and Lear Warner were all involved with the original creation of this book. My thanks to all the *botanica* owners who encouraged and tolerated my teen-aged presence so many years ago and, in essence, helped germinate this book. Thanks also to friends and flamily, especially my children Rachel and Jordan, without whose incredible patience this book would not exist.

about the author

Judika Illes is a spell collector, fortune teller, crisis counselor, and spirit worker. She is the author of *Pure Magic* and *The Element Encyclopedia of 5000 Spells: The Ultimate Reference Book for the Magical Arts.* She lives in New Jersey and conducts workshops across North America. Visit her at www.JudikaIlles.com.

to our reader

Weiser Books, an imprint of Red Wheel/Weiser, publishes books across the entire spectrum of occult and esoteric subjects. Our mission is to publish quality books that will make a difference in people's lives without advocating any one particular path or field of study. We value the integrity, originality, and depth of knowledge of our authors.

Our readers are our most important resource, and we appreciate your input, suggestions, and ideas about what you would like to see published. Please feel free to contact us, to request our latest book catalog, or to be added to our mailing list.

Red Wheel/Weiser, LLC
500 Third Street, Suite 230
San Francisco, CA 94107
www.redwheelweiser.com

Back Cover Material

emergency spells for every occasion

Many spells and charms can take days or even weeks to complete. In *Magic When You Need It,* Judika Illes offers a collection of super-powered magic to help you right now. Is your career in a slump? Are you being visited by ghosts? Short on cash? *Magic When You Need It* can help with these problems and more.

Divided into four sections: Money and Career; Love, Sex, Marriage, and Children; Home; and Trouble, *Magic When You Need It* offers 150 spells to help you find a job, meet your soul mate, protect your home, and many more common (and not so common) predicaments. Using simple instructions and ingredients that can be found in your pantry, combined with easy to find magical oils and botanicals, Illes blends old world and modern magic to provide the reader with safe, effective magical remedies for many of life's troubles. Carry this book in your purse, your car, or keep it on your kitchen counter for accessible magic year round.

Judika Illes is a spell collector, fortune teller, crisis counselor, and spirit worker. She is the author of numerous books including *Pure Magic* and *The Element Encyclopedia of 5000 Spells: The Ultimate Reference Book for the Magical Arts*. She lives in New Jersey and workshops across North America. Visit her at www.JudikaIlles.com.